THE
COCU
CONSENSUS

In Quest of a Church of Christ Uniting

Edited by
Gerald F. Moede

Approved and commended to the churches
by the Sixteenth Plenary of the
Consultation on Church Union

November 30, 1984
Baltimore, Maryland

Copies available from

Consultation on Church Union
Research Park, 151 Wall Street
Princeton, New Jersey 08540-1514

Prices in USA and Canada

Single copies $1.25   plus postage
100-1000 copies $1.00   plus postage
Over 1000 copies $0.75   plus postage

Table of Contents

Introduction

Doctrinal disagreement and dispute have been major factors in the division of the Christian Church since early in its history. As early as the fifties of the first century, the Apostle Paul condemned the grouping of Christians around one or another theological viewpoint, indicating that such behavior was living "according to the flesh," rather than according to the Spirit (I Cor.). In his letter to Philippi he made bold to assert that being of one mind and spirit was an omen of their salvation! Thus the effort to find theological agreement among divided churches is of the utmost importance.

Since 1962 the churches of the Consultation on Church Union have engaged in a serious and inclusive search to find and articulate such agreement. Published steps along the way included *Principles of Church Union* (1966), *A Plan of Union* (1970), and *In Quest of a Church of Christ Uniting* (1976). By 1980 the revised *Quest* document of 1976 was judged mature enough to be sent to the COCU churches for their official response. This 1985 version, accepted in Baltimore, Maryland in November 1984, was revised in accordance with the suggestions made by the churches of the Consultation between 1980 and 1984. We need to express thanks to the people who worked tirelessly on this text in COCU's Theology Commission, with special appreciation to two scholars who chaired it: Professor John Deschner and Dean Lewis Mudge.

It should be noted that the evolution of COCU's maturing consensus took place in recognition of, and correspondence with, the development of the *Baptism, Eucharist, and Ministry* agreement of the Faith and Order Commission of the World Council of Churches. It will therefore be able to contribute to the conciliar fellowship being sought in the WCC.

The Consultation on Church Union is committed to a wider unity than its present nine bodies, although the agreement was drafted primarily by representatives of the present member churches. But a foretaste of the wider constituency is represented by the presence on the COCU Theology Commission of members of the Roman Catholic, Lutheran, and Reformed Church in America communions.

Of vital importance in our growing life together is COCU's attempt to incorporate the theological insights of black Christians, women, and of persons with disabilities. These concerns are now understood to be church-dividing, and they must be addressed, agreed upon, and acted on if the unity of Christians is to fulfill its place in the healing of the divisions of humankind.

The basic questions being posed to the churches in this document should be kept in the readers' minds. We are not inquiring whether this is an adequate Methodist, Episcopal, Presbyterian (or other tradition) statement.

Rather (see page 2), the question we are asking is, "Do you recognize in this text an expression . . . of the Apostolic faith, order, worship, and witness of the Church?" Further, this document should be read in the context of "covenanting," which is the "larger picture" of coming together being proposed in COCU for the reconciliation of the churches during the years immediately before us. (A companion volume describes this process.)

The remainder of the century will represent a true *kairos* for the reconciliation of Christians and churches. If the national bodies of the nine communions of COCU are able to respond affirmatively to this text, an era of deepening common life can develop, and a new "omen of salvation" (in the words of Paul) will be visible.

May this agreement, the fruit of many years of growth and nourishment, be claimed and harvested, and enable us to live in such harmony with one another, that together we may with one voice glorify God (Rom. 15:6) and thus live in accord with the will of Christ Jesus, who makes us one.

Epiphany, 1985
Gerald F. Moede
General Secretary

Preface

With confidence that the Holy Spirit is doing a significant work in our midst, the Theology Commission commends this consensus document to the nine member churches of COCU and to the wider Christian world.

The dialogue and drafting which have led to this statement began, in a formal sense, in 1974. Even then this work stood, and still stands, on the shoulders of those who have worked in the ecumenical vineyard over the decades. We have learned much from Faith and Order, from the bilateral dialogues, and, of course, from COCU's own history. At every stage, this document has been shared with the COCU member churches as well as with observer representatives of other bodies. The responses received have been carefully taken into account.

Our drafting has also been concurrent with that of the *Baptism, Eucharist and Ministry* convergence document of the World Council of Churches, and a certain amount of cross-fertilization has naturally occurred. The present writer, for example, served in both these enterprises. Specific debts to BEM are acknowledged in the present text.

We call this text a "consensus" statement, in comparison with BEM's term "convergence." Rightly, BEM reserves the word "consensus" for a situation of full sharing of faith and life among the churches. An agreed text produced by a committee of theologians is not yet a "consensus" in this sense. We use the word "consensus" here somewhat proleptically but with genuine trust that there may come to be, as a result of this effort, what that word properly implies. This document has been adopted by the delegations of the nine churches as a theological basis for just such sharing. Unlike BEM, it is part of a particular thrust toward the unity of the Church. That explains its length, and in certain respects its specificity.

Already the headline writers are calling the unity we seek here a "merger." That is not the right word. It smacks too much of corporate gigantism. The intent of "covenanting" is to create a situation in which we can grow together with full respect for our respective traditions, gifts, and yes, peculiarities. The right of the different churches to carry into this relationship what is dear to them is very important. The intent of this consensus document will not be understood unless it is read in the context of the process of which it is a part. For more information on this see the *Foreword* and the note at the beginning of Chapter 7.

I take this opportunity to thank the many persons — Commission members, observers, consultants, staff — who have been part of this effort over the years. Their names are listed at the back of this book. At the risk of seeming invidious, I would like to mention especially the two persons who have been continuously part of this work from the very beginning until now. They are Professors J. Robert Nelson and Richard A. Norris. Their contribution, through innumerable drafts and redrafts, has been more than competent and eminently selfless. I would also mention Prof. John Deschner, who served as the first Chairperson of the Commission, and who guided this work through its indispensable early stages.

Lewis S. Mudge
Chair
Theology Commission

Foreword

This document is the first of three parts of a proposal of the Consultation on Church Union for enabling the participating churches to continue on their way toward visible unity. The other two parts of the proposal are found in the emerging work of the Consultation's Commission on Church Order and its Commission on Worship. It is the intent of the Consultation that these parts be understood together. Each constitutes an essential aspect of the process of "covenanting for unity" among the COCU churches: a step in the direction of the ultimate achievement of life together in a Church of Christ Uniting.

This document, THE COCU CONSENSUS: *In Quest of a Church of Christ Uniting*, is being referred by the Consultation to the participating churches for wide study and appropriate action by their highest policy-making bodies. This document will serve as one basis for an emerging covenantal relationship. It is the counsel of the Consultation that ample time be taken for full discussion in each church before the moment of decision is reached, and that the process leading to decision in each church be thoroughly understood by all and coordinated in the fullest possible degree.

The Context of the Covenanting Proposal

In 1970, the Consultation approved and submitted to the participating churches a full Plan of Union. It was clear from the responses of the churches that they were not yet ready to enter immediately into full and organic church union. But neither were they willing to disband the Consultation. Hence, beginning in 1973, the Consultation entered upon a process of "living our way toward unity," through encouraging the development of Generating Communities, Interim Eucharistic Fellowships, and joint study and action. What the Consultation now refers to as "covenanting" is a fuller development of that process.

Covenanting entails a number of deliberate actions by the participating churches. The claiming of this document, THE COCU CONSENSUS, is one of those actions. Other actions of covenanting include a mutual and formal recognition by the participating churches of their respective members, churches, and ministries. There will also be acts designed to reconcile the presently differing forms of ministry, to enable regular eucharistic fellowship, and to create various interim bodies for common life and action at each level of the churches' life. Covenanting, its steps and actions, are more fully described in the report of the Commission on Church Order.

Covenanting, therefore, is an act of solemn commitment to one another by the participating churches. It is embodied in a process of identifying and taking certain mutually agreed actions which will move them toward becoming a visibly united church. The covenanting process is thus a new interim stage in the life of the participating churches together. The act of covenanting does not itself effect visible church union. Formation of one church at this time could prevent our being open to the creative work God may do among us and through us in the process of covenanting. The goal of this process is to let our participating churches become one in the essentials of faith, worship, order, and witness. At the same time, it allows the churches to recognize and embrace the gifts of continued diversity our churches bring in their particular traditions, ethos, and racial and ethnic heritage, while we are spiritually renewed through these relationships and commitments.

By means of this document and the other reports, the Consultation on Church Union now calls its participating churches to a new relationship of commitment which is not yet full and organic union, but which is far more than a consultative relationship such as that which has constituted the life of COCU thus far. The ultimate goal of the Consultation remains: a faithful response to Jesus' call to unity in one visibly united church.

The Meaning of Claiming this Document

This document, THE COCU CONSENSUS: *In Quest of a Church of Christ Uniting*, is a key element in the covenanting process. Therefore, it is important to understand what the act of "claiming" it means.

The 16th Plenary adopted the following resolution:

> RESOLVED: that the 16th (1984) Plenary of the Consultation on Church Union approves this text and asks the participating churches, by formal action, to recognize in it
>
> 1) an expression, in the matters with which it deals, of the Apostolic faith, order, worship, and witness of the Church,
> 2) an anticipation of the Church Uniting which the participating bodies, by the power of the Holy Spirit, wish to become, and
> 3) a sufficient theological basis for the covenanting acts and the uniting process proposed at this time by the Consultation.

The three purposes stated in this resolution should be held firmly in mind. The churches are asked to find in this document "an expression" of the great Apostolic tradition they hold in common, an anticipation of what they intend together to become, and an expression of those things "sufficient" to make next steps in covenanting possible. Each body should be able to find the Apostolic faith reflected here.

As the churches consider their actions with regard to the process of claiming, the following points are to be considered:

1) The document, THE COCU CONSENSUS, is intended to build confidence in the process of covenanting. It is also intended to encourage the development of a common language for the expression of a common faith.

2) The question before each church is, "Do you recognize in this text an expression of the faith of the Church?" The question is not, "How does this consensus agree or disagree with our particular communion's theology?"

3) Consensus as used here does not imply complete unanimity or uniformity of doctrinal understanding. "Consensus" does, however, point toward that fuller confession of our common faith that can be made only on the basis of life together within one ecclesial fellowship.

4) It is important to remember that this consensus is "emerging"; it is an ecumenical witness of a group of churches that are on a pilgrimage of faith and reconciliation.

A Note on Matters of Terminology

An attempt has been made to use terminology consistently throughout the consensus statement. The term "participating churches" is used, as the By-Laws direct, to refer to churches officially related to COCU, and therefore as accepting its aim to "explore" the establishment of a "uniting church" (By-Laws II and III).

In the 1980 edition of this consensus, the term "uniting churches" (plural) was used "with great discretion," for it was desired not to suggest, in a loose manner, commitment to aspects of a plan of union by the participating churches prior to their own decisions. This discretion in the use of terms is still important. But there is need now for a term with which to refer to the state of affairs which will exist when the participating churches, by "claiming" this consensus within the context of a Covenant, agree to live together in ways which will envision the sort of unity the document describes. At the moment they adopt the Covenant, and thereby commit themselves to a series of steps leading to the establishment of Councils of Oversight, the participating churches will become "uniting churches."

This document has adopted the term "Church Uniting" to refer to the union COCU hopes to achieve, with emphasis on its continued openness to new participating churches. This term replaces, throughout, the former term "uniting church." The new term has the advantage of referring to the body which is the eventual goal of this effort by an abbreviated form of its intended proper name, *The Church of Christ Uniting.*

I
Why Unity?

1) Division in the life of the Church is a contradiction of its very nature. Christ's reconciling work is one, and members of the Church fail as Christ's ambassadors in reconciling the world to God if they have not been visibly reconciled to one another.

2) The means by which the good news is preached must be congruous with the content of the good news: a "making whole," a healing of all things in Christ Jesus. The Church, as described in the Bible, is to be a family created by God in Christ out of all tribes and nations and peoples, a family set by God as a sign to the world of the direction in which all creation and history are moving: the summing up of all things in Christ and the coming of the reign of God.

The Imperative for Unity

3) The reasons for seeking unity among the churches are found in the Bible, in Tradition, and in the imperatives of witness and world-wide mission. Unity is a characteristic of the Church into which we are called by Christ's gospel; unity is a characteristic of the vision of the Church held by the great saints and theologians over the centuries. For the Church to be a concrete embodiment of Christ's message and an authentic witness of Christ's mission to the contemporary world, some visible expression of unity is indispensable. Let us consider each of these areas of concern in turn.

4) The New Testament repeatedly affirms the essential, the intrinsic, unity of Christ's Church. In John 17, Jesus prays for his people "that they may all be one . . . so that the world may believe that thou hast sent me" (Jn. 17:21); thus the unity desired is both a harmony of mind and spirit, and a form which is visible to the world, capable of sustaining the life and mission of the body of Christ (I Cor. 12:12-31).

5) Similarly, in John 11 we have already been told that Jesus should die, not for the nation of Israel only "but to gather into one the children of God who are scattered abroad" (Jn. 11:52). Paul enjoins the Philippians to "stand firm in one spirit, with one mind striving side by side for the faith of the gospel" (Phil. 1:27). Such unity is an omen or sign of their salvation from God (Phil. 1:28). To the Galatians Paul writes that they, despite being of different theological persuasions, must eat together as a sign of their unity

in the gospel (Gal. 2:11-16). The Corinthians, as Paul sees them, are denying the gospel by gathering around party names, saying " 'I belong to Paul,' or 'I belong to Apollos,' or 'I belong to Cephas,' or 'I belong to Christ.' " The apostle's rejoinder is swift: "Is Christ divided? Was Paul crucified for you?" (I Cor. 1:12-13) And Paul takes up the argument again two chapters later: "For while there is jealousy and strife among you, are you not of the flesh and behaving like ordinary men? For when one says 'I belong to Paul,' and another 'I belong to Apollos,' are you not merely men? What then is Apollos? What then is Paul? Servants through whom you believed, as the Lord assigned to each. I planted, Apollos watered, but God gave the growth" (I Cor. 3:3-6).

6) Finally, all Christians acknowledge their membership in a community of *one* Lord, *one* faith, *one* baptism, and *one* God (Eph. 4:5a). This is why, with many others, "we believe that the unity which is both God's will and his gift to his Church is being made visible as all in each place who are baptized into Jesus Christ and confess him as Lord and Saviour are brought by the Holy Spirit into one fully committed fellowship, holding the one apostolic faith, preaching the one Gospel, breaking the one bread, joining in common prayer, and having a corporate life reaching out in witness and service to all and who at the same time are united with the whole Christian fellowship in all places and all ages in such wise that ministry and members are accepted by all, and that all can act and speak together as occasion requires for the tasks to which God calls his people" (*The New Delhi Report*, p. 116).

7) The post-biblical Tradition also witnesses powerfully to the essential unity of the Church given in Jesus Christ. The oneness of the Church was early recognized as one of its four "marks," the others being apostolicity, catholicity, and holiness. We find this, for example, in the Nicene (i.e., Constantinopolitan) Creed: "We believe . . . in one holy, catholic and apostolic Church. We confess one baptism for the remission of sins . . . ." Scholars and church leaders also speak forcefully for unity; for example, Ignatius of Antioch exhorted the Ephesians that they should "form a choir, so that joining the symphony by your concord and by your unity, taking your keynote from God, you may with one voice through Jesus Christ sing a song to the Father." Irenaeus of Lyons described the Church as "having received this (apostolic) preaching and this faith, although scattered throughout the world, yet as if occupying but one house, carefully preserves it." Similarly, Cyprian of Carthage emphasized that "God is one, and Christ is one, and his Church is one; one is the faith, and one the people cemented together by harmony into the strong unity of a body."

Historic Sources of Division

8) Despite such affirmations, divisions appeared early in the history of the Church and have multiplied in subsequent centuries. Even in apostolic times, divisions occurred between Jewish and Gentile Christians. In medieval times, schism occurred between Eastern and Western Christians.

Differing doctrinal formulations were not the only causes of these divisions. Discord and disunity also resulted from political preferences, cultural differences, social and economic polarizations, and various forms of discrimination on the basis of race, sex, physical or mental condition, and age.

9) Even as these divisions appeared, many in the Church struggled to maintain and restore Christian unity. Today a world-wide effort has begun to discern the meaning of the unity that Christ intended, and to recover, or to achieve for the first time, such unity on a global basis.

10) There are many reasons why efforts toward unity have become a vital concern in the twentieth century. Perhaps the most important single reason is a growing consciousness of the sinfulness of division. The disunity of the Church is a stumbling block to the world. It is a scandal that calls into question the being of God and the resurrection of Christ, and so imperils the credibility of the gospel. A united church will be able to develop a more nearly responsible ecumenical strategy which will give a more credible witness in the world. A united church will be more able to exert a genuinely transforming force in society. For example, the injustices which hinder peace among nations and which threaten the very survival of humankind are in part the inevitable effect of disunity upon the Church's social mission.

11) Secondly, the revolution in communications and increased mobility of large numbers of people have raised the churches' awareness of Christian communions other than their own. But still more important has been the impact of religious pluralism. No longer can it be assumed that all the people in a given area are Christian; no longer is there the luxury of "one church for every theological viewpoint." "Christendom" is gone; everywhere Christians are in a missionary situation. Christians must find a way of being together in such a way that the very form of the Church in the world will communicate its message to the world, and still make room, within consensus, for a great range of theological points of view, practices in worship, and forms of organization.

12) Thirdly, after the church union in Canada (1925), the real impact of our now universal missionary situation was largely felt outside Europe and North America. It is here that the most extensive and successful church unions have been achieved, especially in India, certain parts of Africa, Asia, and Australia. In these regions it became evident by the early twentieth century that transplanted church divisions made little sense. Not only were the issues involved hard to express, or even irrelevant, in such new countries and cultures, but it became clear that Christians could not invite people of other religions to recognize and follow Jesus as their Lord and Savior when they themselves, by their divisions, were proclaiming that they did not believe in his sufficiency to reconcile all people in one body to God. Today Christians are learning from these "mission fields" that the "household" they exhibit to the world is an indispensable vehicle of witness.

Contemporary Church-Dividing Issues

13) Unity today is a task that requires resolution not only of old but also of new divisions. Divisions must be overcome between the different forms of catholicism and protestantism. But there is also need for a reconciliation of long-standing estrangements in the Church which now have surfaced in forms echoing tensions in the modern world: estrangements between the sexes, and among races, cultures, classes, political opinions, and visions of the meaning of justice.

14) Divisions of this sort are of central concern to the Consultation on Church Union. By its very nature the Consultation stands against every sort of division in the Church of Jesus Christ. Often that division has been viewed only in terms of disagreement in such matters as the sacraments, ministry, or church order. But these things do not exist in a vacuum. The Church participates in, and reflects, the sources of division between human beings in society and culture. COCU was born at a time, the early sixties, when the United States was being compelled to reach a new consciousness concerning the feelings of alienation experienced by a number of its citizens: at a time when this country could no longer pretend that certain of its historic inequities were non-existent.

15) Early in the Consultation's life, moreover, it was joined by three major historic branches of Black Methodism. The racism which brought about the existence of these churches is one of the grave sins of persons and religious institutions in the United States. There are other churches within the COCU communions which arose historically as racially/ethnically separated churches. These churches arose despite being ignored by the larger community of faith and flourished as language-speaking churches. They often attached themselves to existing denominations and communions but to this day remain alienated. These churches — along with minority members of the other COCU churches — bring to the Consultation a distinctive perspective on theology and ethics, on ecclesiology and the Kingdom. Thus they keep the Consultation aware of the relevance of these distinctive perspectives to the work that needs to be done to rid ourselves of the sin of racism. Furthermore, in several successive drafts of this Consensus, a series of warnings concerning the church-dividing potential of such realities as racism, sexism, institutionalism, and congregational exclusivism have appeared as appendices called "Alerts."

Much more work needs to be done in defining institutionalism and congregational exclusivism.* However, the matters of racism, sexism, and prejudice against persons with disabilities are now addressed throughout this text. Statements regarding these problems will be found particularly in the treatments of creation in the image of God, and of the new creation into which Christians enter by Baptism. Nevertheless, these issues need to be discussed at this point in the document because of their relevance to every element in it.

---

*Work on these issues lies outside the scope, but not the concern of the present document, and is referred by the 16th Plenary to The Commission on Church Order.

16) "One way of describing these issues," the original authors of the Alerts wrote, "would be to say that our deepest differences reach beyond sacraments and ministry into the divisions that tragically separate the human family." But such differences "are themselves theological in that they distort God's plan to bring all creation together, everything in heaven and on earth, with Christ as head" (Eph. 1:10).

[a] Where racism is concerned, the Alerts asked, "Why ought we expect to be brothers and sisters of equal status in the Church of Christ Uniting when members of the majority refuse to live next door as neighbors? How can we have 'brotherhood' and 'sisterhood' without neighborhood?" While COCU documents insist on equal representation and voice for racial and ethnic communities, "Black Christians and churches have observed or experienced the divisive and demoralizing consequences of merger for the black experience, institutions, and community. Many Blacks feel that integration or merger causes fundamental and serious disruptions resulting in the elimination of leadership and loss of black self-control, absorption and the loss of identity, accommodation and the loss of self-reliance. And while some of these are offered up in the body of Christ, it all too often is assumed that they must not be given up in the body of white Christianity. Blacks ask, "If a church is not willing to risk too much of itself prior to union on the scale envisioned by COCU, will it practice equality and representation *after* union in matters of race, sex, and age?"

[b] As for the issue of sexism, the language of the Alerts is equally striking. "The most subtle and significant threat sexism poses for the future of COCU is the possibility of a loss of new life — the new life, the gift of God, that is being generated by the movement of women and men into full partnership in the task of creating a new human community." And again, "COCU's task in relation to sexism is urgent because the loss of new life has already begun. Growing numbers of women and men who are committed to liberating styles of human partnerships are becoming unable to participate in the life of the churches as they now exist. These creative Christians can no longer give any legitimacy to the polarizing sexism that permeates the language and practice of worship, theology, styles of ministry, and the governing structures of all denominations. The Consultation may live its way toward union, therefore, only to discover within five or ten years that many of its members have been so alienated along the way that "unity" has become a gentlemen's agreement within the dominant group, rather than an agreement of partners who have struggled together toward true mutuality in every expression of their personal and institutional lives."

[c] Even though none of the Alerts deals specifically with the role of persons with disabilities, this concern has nevertheless been

present in the thinking of the Consultation. Since the Louvain meeting of the World Council of Churches' Faith and Order Commission (1971), full inclusion of persons with disabilities in the life of the Church has been understood as a central, not a peripheral, ecumenical issue. It continues to be so understood in this document. Physical access to facilities is an indispensable starting point, but it is not enough. Subtle patronizing of persons with disabilities, the refusal to receive such sisters and brothers as full human beings and contributing members of Christ's body, is a form of apostasy. It has no place in the Church of Christ Uniting. Such forms of rejection appear not only in attitudes and structures, but also in patterns of language and other forms of communication which convey excluding assumptions. We must be constantly vigilant so that we do not give ground in these matters, as well as loving and creative in our attempt to overcome new obstacles to inclusiveness, as we become aware of them.

17) There is no easy solution to these dilemmas. The Church, however, is called to be a community of reconciliation in the modern world. Hence it must continually find ways of bringing its differing interpretations of the gospel into one community of faith. As a community of hope and love, it must also find means for healing the divisions among people who are alienated as a result of such unchristian attitudes as racism, sexism, ageism, and handicapism. The challenges of the modern world offer new possibilities for seeing and overcoming the old divisions. This includes a mutually enriching appropriation of the theological and spiritual impulses which gave birth to the uniting denominations. Insofar as Christians have been divided from one another, they have suffered by being deprived of each other's gifts, help, and correction. Even when communication must consist of protest or rebuke (e.g., "speaking the truth in love," Eph. 4:15), it cannot be fully accomplished in isolation, but requires visible unity. Further, it is the traditions and practices over which we have become divided that contain the rich diversity of gifts that we must offer to the modern world, gifts whose power for the reconciliation of humankind can be released if we live them out as one People.

II
Unity
A Gift To Be Made Visible

1) The unity of the Church is a gift of God in Jesus Christ to be made visible before the world. Diverse as the People of God are by reasons of race, sex, physical or mental condition, nationality, tongue, politics, vocation, and religious heritage, they belong to one another by their creation in the image of God and by Baptism into the one body of Christ (I Cor. 12:12-13). Just as Christ is one and undivided, so it is essential for his body to be one.

2) Each of the participating churches justifiably seeks to preserve the heart of its heritage and tradition in which it has received gracious gifts from the Lord.

3) The particular traditions, however, have on occasion been distorted by false claims of exclusiveness and even of ultimacy. Thus, while church union involves preservation and sharing, it also requires repentance, conversion, and a new commitment by all to the enrichment coming from the gifts and experience of the other uniting churches. Indeed, for the sake of unity, it may be necessary for a church to modify some of its historic customs in order to incorporate into its life the contributions of other traditions joining in the Church Uniting.

4) That which would be modified in the process of union, if anything, would be upon the decision of the church involved in the change; it would not be imposed from the outside.

5) The Church Uniting may find that it will need the contributions of traditions other than those of the presently participating churches, in order to become visibly a fuller and more diversified community of reconciled persons and gifts. The call is to a new and growingly inclusive form of the Church. In this spirit what is envisioned is a Church Uniting bearing enough family resemblance to the separate traditions to manifest its continuity with them, yet unlike any of the churches in their past separateness.

6) There can be no precise blueprint for the form which a Church Uniting will eventually attain. But inasmuch as the participating churches are already bound by years of Bible study, theological reflection, shared mission, and common prayer, it can be said that the Holy Spirit has led the churches to identify a number of distinctive characteristics that should mark the reconciling and liberating community which is being sought, in

anticipation of which they are already beginning to act. Each of these seven following characteristics is seen as fundamental to the quest for the visible unity of a Church Uniting which is truly catholic, truly evangelical, and truly reformed.

[a] *Celebration of God's grace shall be central to our life together.* Celebration means rendering glory to God and giving joyful expression to the love by which we are bound together. As we celebrate God's grace in Christ, we who were formally strangers offer ourselves back to God as a reconciled family (Eph. 2:12-21). God has provided the very means of grace by which we are forgiven, reconciled to God and one another, renewed in life, and given our common identity and mission. These are the saving gospel of Jesus Christ, the one apostolic faith, the sacraments of Baptism and Eucharist. Through these gifts the Holy Spirit leads us into all truth and empowers us to grow more and more into the likeness of Christ.

[b] *Christ's ongoing mission of salvation for the whole world will mark every endeavor of a Church Uniting.* Salvation is deliverance from sin and entrance into *shalom*: peace with God, health, and liberation. The risen Christ, to whom all power has been given in heaven and on earth, is at once Savior and Lord of persons and of history. The closing words of Jesus as recorded in the Gospel according to Matthew, "Go, therefore!", leave no human sphere outside of God's claim (Matt. 28:18-19a). As servant, the Church's mission is to the whole of human life, societies, and social structures, including individuals and their religious needs. But sin is at work, denying men and women the fruition of their calling as children of God, both within and without the Church, in such practices and attitudes as racism, sexism, ageism, prejudice toward persons with disabilities, institutionalism, and congregational exclusiveness. The Christian faith clearly assumes that converted and baptized individuals become transformed persons. This should mean freedom from discrimination in all relationships, social and institutional, as well as personal. The Church Uniting will take this assumption very seriously in theology and in practice. Since "in Christ God was reconciling the world to himself" (II Cor. 5:19), there are no such things as "off-limits zones" for Christians in mission. At the same time, it ought not to surprise Christians when they find allies for social mission among those who do not confess Christ's name(Mk. 9:38-40).

[c] *Each member of a Church Uniting will be called to an apostolic and priestly ministry.* A mission of such dimensions and promise will require of each member of a Church Uniting an apostolic identity, i.e., the identity of one sent to share with others the experience of wholeness which he or she, and the believing community, have found in Christ (Eph. 4:15-16). This is one of the chief implications of what is called the priesthood of all believers. In a Church Uniting, the distinction between ordained and non-ordained

ministries will not mean the establishment of a ladder of dignities. Rather it will mean the ordering under Christ of the gifts and special callings of all for the sake of the ministry with which all are charged — that of loving and healing the world as Jesus did. In this way a Church Uniting will offer persuasive witness that it is indeed the People of God.

[d] *The structures of a Church Uniting will mirror the diversity of its membership in every aspect of its fellowship and ministry* (III:7b). Its racial and ethnic multiplicity will be held forth both as one of its richest gifts and the most persuasive witness that the reconciliation it offers to the world in the name of Christ is already at work in its midst (I Cor. 12:12-27). The same may be said for the contribution of male and female, of young and old, and of persons with disabilities. A Church Uniting will seek, both within and outside its own fellowship, to redress that imbalance of power and powerlessness which results from the fact that people have been, and are being, oppressed by reason of class, race, sex, age, physical disability, or any other such factor.

[e] *Because of the mutual enrichment of its several traditions, a Church Uniting will more faithfully reflect the universality of the body of Christ.* It is recognized that each of the participating churches, with its particular traditions and history, genuinely manifests the reality of Christ's one body (I Cor. 1:12-13; 3:4-13, 21-22). For this reason, a Church Uniting will value and maintain everything in these separate heritages which serves the gospel. Each particular church will find, by union with the others, not loss but expansion of identity, through giving and receiving in a renewed life of faith, worship, fellowship, and ministry. Yet many forms of church life which are valued as precious or even essential may have to be modified so that a Church Uniting can be born. The new humanity of our Lord's risen body required suffering and death. Participation in that body requires no less. The most painful instance of such dying may be the overcoming of present narrow denominational identities.

[f] *Previous ecumenical relationships shall be maintained and strengthened.* A Church Uniting should be a uniting church. The bonds now existing between the participating churches and other Christian bodies (confessional, conciliar, and the like) will be preserved. A Church Uniting should seek to maintain communion with those churches with which the participating churches now enjoy communion. The unity of Christ's body is indivisible. To manifest it in the local community without expressing it in a broader area would defeat ecumenical aims just as surely as would preoccupation with world denominational or confessional unity alone (Acts 15:1-34). Relationships to other bodies cannot remain separate and private matters, but belong to the whole Church Uniting. The goal of a Church Uniting will be to add to existing associations new relation-

ships which have hitherto been inaccessible to the separated churches, and thus to extend through visible forms and vital experience its solidarity with the People of God in all places and ages.

(i) Because a Church Uniting is only a step toward the reunion of Christ's Church, its commitment is toward a wider unity both within this nation and outside its borders. There is danger in a church organized solely within one nation, since nationalistic attitudes may pervert or silence the judgment of God's Word on the cultural, social, and political shape of national life. Nevertheless a church is sent to the society within which it is called, and apart from this society, it cannot bear true and responsible witness in this world (Gal. 2:7-10).

(ii) The participating churches desire to become more than a new and more inclusive denomination. They seek full reconciliation with all Christian bodies — with those whose separate identities stem from the very ancient divisions, as well as with those of more recent origin. This pilgrimage has as its ultimate goal the unity of the universal Church.

[g] *Maximum openness shall be provided for our continuing renewal and reformation* (III:13). No visible, earthly body, however idealistically planned, can ever be safe from the corruption of human folly, prejudice, ignorance, and sin. From such corruption, God has repeatedly saved the Church through those who under the freedom of the gospel opposed its aberrations, checked its excesses, or summoned it to repentance (Jn. 2:13-22; Gal. 2:11-16). Provision for dissent is essential so that order may not stifle conscience nor prohibit the expression of viewpoints, particularly by minorities, who can easily be ignored or coerced by the majority. Provision for diversity and openness in decision-making sufficient to recognize and include both minority and majority opinions and interest will thus be made. As Christians continue to listen to one another, improvising new structures in the transitional period, building flexibility in the emerging organization, experiencing new ways of worship, and expressing obedience to Christ in joint action in society with all persons of good will, they will awaken to new understandings of the great work God is doing and calling us to share. What is essential is that every possible channel be open by which the purifying action of God's Holy Spirit may be experienced (II Cor. 3:17; Gal. 5:13-25). Power must, then, be checked by vigilant conscience, and authority balanced by accountability. Decisions must be made in the open and shared by the entire body. In so doing, a Church Uniting will come closer to realizing the wholeness, unity, and mission of the pilgrim community of Christ.

III
Toward A Church
Catholic, Evangelical, and Reformed

1) Christ the risen and reigning Lord has one body and many members in this world. These members are all baptized by the one Spirit into his body, the Church (I Cor. 12:13). By dying to their old selves and rising to new life with Christ and in Christ, they belong to the community of suffering and service, of faith, hope, and love which carries Christ's saving mission to all people (Rom. 6:5; Phil. 1:20; I Cor. 13:13). If they will put old divisions behind them, the churches can bear witness to the unity of the Church and its mission by becoming uniting churches. As they press forward to what lies ahead they can become a Church Uniting. Moving in the unity of the Spirit to the unity of faith, they must seek the structural forms and institutions which will make manifest their fundamental oneness in Christ.

2) In what spirit, though, and with what guiding principles, shall this search for an institutional expression of unity in Christ be undertaken? Such a united and uniting body will be truly catholic — that is, to manifest in the forms of its life and action the wholeness of the Christ who is its life. At the same time, such a body will be truly evangelical— that is, to know the Christ in whom it lives as one who is to be received and proclaimed to the world as God's transforming good news. Finally, such a body will be truly reformed — that is, to recognize in Christ, whose identity it shares, one who calls it ever and again to change and to purify its ways.

3) In the history of the Church, to be sure, these three adjectives — "catholic," "evangelical," and "reformed" — have frequently been used to describe separate and sometimes warring traditions. Each of them, however, indicates an essential dimension of the Church's common life in Christ; and for just that reason the Church Uniting will strive to embody in its life and structures the qualities to which these terms refer.

Truly Catholic

4) "Catholicity" means universality, inclusiveness, unity. The Church is catholic, then, to the extent that it has these characteristics (Eph. 4:4-5).

5) The catholicity of the Church is rooted in the fact that it is a People whose shared life is a participation, through the Spirit, in the person and work of Jesus Christ.

6) The Church treasures its essential institutions — the Scriptures and the exposition of them; common and individual prayer and praise; confession of God in Christ through the Spirit. By these means Christians know and receive the "grace and truth" of the Word made flesh (Jn. 1:14) and so enter on a new kind of existence. As catholic, therefore, the Church is not ashamed to value and even to venerate these visible and human institutions, because they are also the means by which it lives in Christ.

7) For the Church to be catholic, then, means for it to embody and express in the forms of its life and action the fulness of the Christ who is "our wisdom, our righteousness and sanctification and redemption" (I Cor. 1:30). Thus the idea of catholicity includes the following components:

[a] The Church catholic manifests Christ's *universality*. Each local church — itself the Church catholic in its own place — is a part of the greater communion of saints which extends over the whole world and throughout all ages. Each assembly of Christians shares the calling, the problems, and the faith of other such assemblies in other times and places, and from their witness it learns and is built up (I Cor. 14:12), even as it makes its own witness and its own contribution to the life of the whole body. In this sense, to be catholic means to be in spiritual, intellectual, and institutional communion with all others who share or have shared the calling of God in Christ, and thus to live in a fellowship of mutual affection, responsibility, and correction.

[b] The Church catholic, because it lives in the new humanity which is the risen Christ, is *inclusive*. As Jesus' ministry embraced all and was directed in a special way to those whom the world rejected, so the Church embraces those who are adjudged of little value by the world, regardless of distinctions of sex, race, physical or mental condition, nationality, or social rank (I Cor. 1:26-31). All members are given the same gift of faith and the same promise of the gospel, attested and sealed in Baptism. All share in the life and work of the Church, having a common identity and forming a single people in Christ (II:6,d). Hence the Church catholic is comprehensive in its capacity to embrace and sustain diversity in the expression of its faith and of its life of witness and service. Refusing deadening conformity and sterile uniformity, it welcomes the full range of the gifts which the Holy Spirit distributes among it members (I Cor. 12:4-11) just as it values the varieties of natural endowment in sex, race, age, physical or mental condition, culture, and linguistic or ethnic identity (IV:6).

[c] The Church catholic lives in the *one faith* which was delivered by the witnessing apostles to the first Christians, and which has been kept in continuity ever since (Jude 3; Gal. 1:9, 12). The meaning of this faith can be, and has been, expressed in a variety of legitimate ways (V:8-9). The Church, however, because it lives and understands itself only through the nurture and disciplines of the authentic apostolic witness, guards continually against distortion and denial of this foundation. The apostolic faith and witness is binding

and normative just because it points always to Jesus Christ, who is ever faithful and ever present. The Church's rich and many-sided continuity of confession is maintained within the community by faithful preaching of the Word and celebration of the sacraments. It is maintained beyond the community by the mission and ministries of its members.

[d] *Corporate discipline* in Christian life and teaching is necessary to maintain and nurture the catholic integrity of the Church (IV:14). Christian freedom comes as a gift in and with the gospel, delivering people from servitude to self and bondage to the alienating and destructive powers of sin. Such freedom, however, is experienced in the shape of a new kind of servitude — servitude to the power of love (Gal. 5:1, 13), and in fidelity to the truth (II Cor. 13:8).

(i) Constrained by the love of Christ (II Cor. 5:14), members who are entrusted with responsibility and authority for preserving the integrity of the Church need at the same time to seek the restitution and welfare of the failing member (Gal. 6:1-2; Heb. 12:7-11; James 5:19-20). Nevertheless attitudes, words, and actions that are clearly contrary to the truth which is in Christ, or injurious to the life and mission of the community, must be judged and corrected.

(ii) The Church catholic has established means by which appropriate discipline may be exercised: the normative canon of Scriptures, presenting the will of God revealed in Christ; an acknowledged rule of faith and life aimed at growth in grace; a theological tradition which freely and continually reinterprets the faith for effective mission; transmission of ministerial responsibility; faith for effective mission; and constitutions and canons for maintaining order and wholeness.

8) The Church catholic stands within a form of the world which is passing away. Nevertheless it affirms the significance in God's sight of that world's common life in all of its dimensions. It values in that world everything which is of God's creation and seeks to inform the whole realm of culture and society with the spirit of the redeeming Christ. In those who hear its message it inspires new vision — for political and social order, for philosophical understanding, as well as for literature, music, and the visual arts. Because the world is made in Christ and for him, the Church catholic accepts the fact that it is of the world and responsible in and for it.

Truly Evangelical

9) The evangelical character of the Church means that it is constantly informed and empowered by the Gospel of Jesus Christ, and that it is commissioned to share its message of new life and hope with all people (Jn. 17:17-21). By initiation into faith, Christians are, in a true sense, ordained to a caring priesthood and to a company of witnesses to Christ (VII:28). Spreading the good news in ways which speak to the varieties of the human

condition, the Church offers new possibilities and resources for both individuals and institutions (I Tim. 2:1-4). It conveys the sure promise that God forgives, reconciles, heals, and calls us to a new order of life in the risen Lord. Despite its own shortcomings, of which it constantly repents, the Church holds forth this news and this promise, and endeavors to realize and embody them in its communal life.

10) Being truly evangelical, the Church will manifest certain characteristic emphases:

[a] *The Gospel means Jesus Christ.* Christ is both its bearer and its content. Recognizing this, the Church repeats Jesus' own message of the present and coming reign of God, with all of its radical requirements and hopeful promises (Mk. 1:14-15). This continuing recital of Jesus' message to the world is at the same time complemented by witness to his ministry, suffering, death, resurrection, and saving power (I Cor. 2:2). The evangelical faith and message touch upon every dimension of human experience, but in every point they confess Jesus Christ as Lord.

[b] *The Scriptures have authority.* The Scriptures are the normative authority for knowledge of Jesus Christ and of God's dealing with the people of Israel and the Church (Jn. 5:39). That authority, understood in the light of the living Tradition (V:6) and reasoned exegesis, and illumined by the Holy Spirit, always remains primal and effectual (I Cor. 11:2, 15:1-11). The Church lives by the promises of God in the Bible and stands under God's judgment and discipline.

[c] *Through the working of the Holy Spirit the Church evangelical experiences the power of the gospel in its own life.* The Spirit seals God's promise in the hearts of believers (Eph. 1:13-14). The Spirit conforms the life of individual and community to that of Christ (Rom. 8:1-17). By this work of the Spirit the Church is separated from the idolatries of this world, and built up in love through the gifts and charisms given its members (Jn. 4:1-3; I Cor. 12:1-11). The mark of its life is thus mutual participation in the gifts of God: in the presence and fruit of the Holy Spirit, in the prayers of common worship and the communion of Christ's Body and Blood, in the suffering which comes with service and witness, and in the joys and hopes of the new life in Christ (Gal. 5:22-23; Acts 2:42-44; I Cor. 10:16-17).

[d] God's mission to the world through Jesus Christ and the Holy Spirit has become *the evangelical mission of the Church.* The mandate for mission is for the whole Church, in every place, by every member. Mission and evangelism are inseparable, just as there is no antithesis between action and word (Jn. 3:21; I Jn. 1:6). Even during his earthly ministry Jesus began sending his disciples with the power to preach and to heal (Mk. 6:7). As the risen Lord, he commissioned them to share the gospel and the power of the Spirit (Jn. 20:21-23; Acts 1:8). In the centuries which have followed, the purpose of this

mission has remained the same: that all people and nations may hear the gospel and respond by faith in Jesus Christ as the incarnate, serving, crucified, risen, and exalted Lord, and may know the transforming power of Christ in their individual and common lives.

11) The gospel is not only heard. It is seen and experienced in actions which are sacrificial, redemptive, and empowering (Matt. 5:16). Through the Spirit's enabling presence, such actions are addressed to the whole range of human need. Personal and individual needs are met by sharing goods, showing care, offering community in love, and exemplifying forgiveness and hope (Matt. 25:35-40). Social needs are met by struggling to overcome oppression and exploitation, by working for human liberation and for justice, and by taking economic and political action to correct inequities in the distribution of life's necessities (Micah 6:8; Lk. 4:17-21; Matt. 23:23).

12) In all these ways the Church evangelical is employed by God, who acts through it for the welfare and salvation of the whole human family, and for the redemption of all creation (Rom. 8:19-23). In all these ways, the Church keeps inviting people to believe, receive, and celebrate God's work.

Truly Reformed

13) To say that the Church is truly reformed is to recognize that Christ continually calls it to repentance and reform. As the Church is sustained by the Holy Spirit, it preserves continuity, through its form of doctrine, polity, and ministry, with the Church of all times and places. These traditional forms, however, are always subject to critical judgment which asks about their conformity and usefulness to the apostolic Gospel of Jesus Christ. In this way the Church, both in its reality and in its appearance, is constantly being reformed, and is always to be reformed, by the Word of God (Rev. 3:14-22; Gal. 3:1-5). Whether in the manner of the papal and monastic reforms of the Middle Ages, the evangelical Reformation of the sixteenth century, the evangelical revivals of the eighteenth and nineteenth centuries, the global reformation represented by the ecumenical movement of the twentieth century, or the numerous local and regional movements for purification and renewal, the Word of God is never without effect on the Church (Isaiah 55:10-11; Heb. 4:12). What then are the marks of a Church truly reformed?

[a] Drawing an analogy from the nomadic tribes of desert lands, the Bible portrays the Church as a *people on pilgrimage* (I Cor. 10:1-4; Heb. 11:29, 37 – 12:2). This analogy is not meant to point simply to geographical movement; rather, it suggests the Church's restless quest for the realization of God's reign (Matt. 6:10). As the people of Israel were called and led by the Lord through the wilderness and into a promised land, so the Church is on the move in history, anticipating that "city which has foundations, whose builder and maker is God" (Heb. 11:10). When the Church is called a pilgrim People, however, equal emphasis falls on both words in this phrase. The pilgrims are

truly *a People*, the People of God reconstituted in Christ (Rom. 9:6-8; Gal. 6:16; Eph. 2:11-13; I Pet. 2:9-10). The Church is capable of "pitching its tent" in every place and culture. Yet as a pilgrim People it can never be fully at home in any place (Phil. 3:20; Heb. 13:13-14). This means, in modern terms, that the Church must not become encrusted in traditionalism or carry unnecessary ecclesiastical baggage. It means also that Christianity cannot become a culture-religion, or a civil religion, or a nationalistic and imperialistic cult.

[b] The Church reformed expects to stand under the constant *judgment of God*, even in its identity as the body of Christ. By reason of its special vocation, it is the place where divine judgment begins (I Pet. 4:17). Everything treasured by the Church — attitudes and institutions, customs and practices — are constantly re-examined and reconstituted for the sake of greater faithfulness in thought, life, and work. The Church must accept this judgment responsibly. It must practice self-examination without self-justification, and self-criticism without self-repudiation. The judgment of God's Word finds its fruit in creative discontent, rooted in the conviction that a pilgrim People is one which continually grows in grace and fidelity. Because the Holy Spirit precedes the Church in its mission, the Church is ready to accept new forms and expressions of life and faith.

[c] The reformed Church is always a *servant Church*. Only a community which resists and rejects temptations to self-exaltation and grandeur can assume "the form of a servant" as Jesus Christ did (Phil. 2:1-11). No admonition about the true nature of discipleship, whether for the community or for individuals, is more clearly conveyed in Scripture than this. Christians have always regarded Jesus's humiliation and death on the cross as a supreme act of servanthood, enacting quite literally the prophecy about the servant of God in Isaiah 53 (I Pet. 2:22-24). The Church, then, can carry out its prophetic function in human society only insofar as it is ready to experience the sacrifices and share the abuses accorded the oppressed.

[d] To be reformed by the Word of God means *to be renewed* for God's future and not only to be reprimanded for past sins. The Church has a vigorous memory (II:6,g). It remembers with encouragement its past fidelities, but it recalls as well its dreadful apostasies in both faith and action. For the latter it must accept God's judgment and forgiveness, and then, "forgetting what lies behind and straining forward to what lies ahead" (Phil. 3:13), place full confidence in the God who makes all things new (Rev. 21:5). To be reformed, then, means that the Church corporately, and its members individually, need continually to be reconverted to God in faithfulness to the gospel.

14) The passing of outmoded forms and ways heralds the expectation and coming of *the new creation* for any persons who are in Christ (II Cor. 5:17). The pilgrim Church, subject to judgment and open to transformation, partakes of that new creation; it lives in tension between the already and the

not yet (Lk. 11:20; Matt. 6:10). In many ways the Church is thus already catholic (affirming its apostolic rootage and seeking to be inclusive), evangelical (under the rule of Scripture and engaged in God's mission), and reformed (open to judgment and renewal of life and faith). But in none of these dimensions can it be said yet to express fully what God intends. God's promise to the Church is that it will become Christ's body on earth more authentically, God's pilgrim People in mission more zealously, God's partner in covenant more faithfully. The Church thus lives in joyous anticipation of God's reign over all people.

15) The Church can be a sign or foretaste of this Kingdom to the extent that it willingly subjects itself to reform (I Cor. 11:26-27). The time of the Church in history is between the times of life, death, and resurrection of Jesus Christ and his final coming in glory. In proclamation, celebration, fellowship, common life, and mission the Church invites all men and women to participate in provisional experience of the destiny which Christ its head offers to all. God calls the Church between these times to be faithful and loving in building up the body of Christ, in witnessing to the gospel and engaging in the total mission to all persons and institutions, and indeed to the whole of creation. As long as the Church is responsive to this call, it will lead persons to faith and salvation, and "the powers of death will not prevail against it" (Matt. 16:18).

IV
Membership

The Unity of the Body and the Diversity of Its Members

1) The word "member," in Christian understanding, derives from the Apostle Paul's image of "the body of Christ," into which we are incorporated by faith through Baptism. "Now you are the body of Christ and individually members of it" (I Cor. 12:27). Through incorporation as members into this body, we receive our identity as Christians (I Cor. 12:12-13; Rom. 6:3-4; Gal. 2:20). As the human being has many parts, so this body has many individual members, each of whom is valuable to the work of Christ, who is the head of the one body and the source of its unity (Col. 1:18).

2) Concretely, membership involves entrance into a visible community of believers in a given locality, with a corresponding recognition of that community as a particular realization of the universal body of Christ. Membership in the body of Christ and in any given community of believers is voluntary in the sense that faith, as response to God's initiative, is a free act, and in the sense that membership is developed by willing participation in the Church's ministry and witness.

3) Among these members, there are varieties of gifts, but the same Spirit, varieties of service, but the same Lord, varieties of working, but the same God who inspires them all in every one (I Cor. 12:4-6). This God-given diversity of talent and calling in its members is essential both to the Church's mission and to its unity as a living body (Eph. 4:11-16), (III:7,b). Moreover, such differences as those of race, sex, age, physical or mental condition, tongue, and nationality manifest the richness of Christ's purpose in creation and redemption (Rom. 10:11-13; Eph. 2:11-15; Rev. 21:24).

4) This diversity, too, therefore, must not merely be acknowledged and admitted, but appreciated as treasures with which God has endowed the Church. Rather than ignoring or suppressing such differences, Christians have the privilege of cherishing them. They must resist the temptation to discriminate and divide (James 2:1-5). They must permit the controversy which such diversity occasions to find its just and proper issue in fellowship (Eph. 4:15). They must insure that no one is deprived of place or participation. In this way, because of the grace by which they are already at one in Christ, believers must bear witness in a divided world to the richly diversified unity which God intends for human society under his Word.

5) While the Church celebrates diversity, it does not forget that in

23

Christ Jesus there are no longer distinctions to be made on the basis of race, gender, physical, mental, or social condition (Gal. 3:28). The Church cannot permit practices in its corporate life which betray this oneness in Christ.

6) Membership in the Church, therefore, is for all persons who receive and believe the gospel (III:7,b). The Church has all too often practiced discrimination against racial minorities, women, the young and old, socially marginal and persons with disabilities, and others who are oppressed. Consequently, a vigorous struggle must be waged against all such abuses of human diversity, within the Church itself as well as in the larger society. The Church Uniting will receive into membership persons with developmental or accidental disabilities whose only response in faith may be spiritual or mystical, but in the sight of God real and dynamic.

Membership in the Body

7) To be a Christian is to be a member of the community of Christian faith. The word "membership" is commonly used in several senses — incorporation into the body of Christ as the one Church universal, enrollment in one of the particular churches in the divided state of the one Church universal, and participation in a local parish or congregation of a specific church. Both within and among the churches there exists a variety of conceptions about how these meanings are interconnected. The full meaning of life together with Jesus Christ and with one another exceeds the limited conceptions which the churches, in their divisions, have devised. The Church Uniting will not grant exclusive validity, or impose on anyone an obligation, to any of those specific historical conceptions. It does affirm that membership in a particular church is membership in the whole People of God. The Church Uniting will dedicate itself to the removal of any and all impediments in its life which prevent it from receiving into full membership all members of the particular churches.

8) Scripture gives a rich and varied picture of the meaning and implications of this membership. Because they are united to Jesus Christ in his living body, the Church's members are united to one another and grow together by the power of the Holy Spirit in the bond of peace (Eph. 4:15-16). Because the members care for one another, all suffer together if even one member suffers; and if one member is honored, all rejoice together (I Cor. 12:26). Because all are children in the household of God, they are constrained by love to live as brothers and sisters, and also, as they accept divine discipline and instruction, to express their love for God in worship and work (Eph. 2:19-22). Because all are members of a priestly people, whose High Priest is Christ alone, they are endowed with varieties of gifts for the exercise of service to one another and to all people (I Pet. 2:9; Heb. 10:19-25; I Cor. 12:7). Because they are the universal People of God, they are commissioned to proclaim and share the gospel, and to be a leavening influence for reconciliation among peoples and nations (Matt. 28:18-20). Since God sent the Son so that we might realize in him that human oneness

STUDY GUIDE

Helps for Studying

THE COCU CONSENSUS:
In Quest of a Church of Christ Uniting

Janet Penfield and Robert K. Welsh

Introduction

THE COCU CONSENSUS was adopted by the nine denominational delegations at the last Plenary of the Consultation on Church Union in November, 1984, after more than twenty years in the making. It was then referred to the churches to "receive" or to "claim" as their own. For this reception to be honest and meaningful, the document will need to be studied and known as widely as possible throughout the communions.

To help this process we offer this *Study Guide* so that groups at various levels of the churches can devote time and effort to understanding the heart of the agreement. In these pages the major developments in theological agreement which seek to overcome previous church-dividing issues are noted and discussed.

Five sessions are outlined for the overall study. Each should be planned for at least 1½ hours, so that meaningful and in-depth discussion may take place. If more time for study is desired, a sixth session can easily be added. It is suggested that study groups be composed denominationally but including persons from as many of the COCU communions as possible. In this way misunderstandings and easy caricatures can be avoided. If the group is composed of persons from more than one congregation, we suggest that the first session be planned primarily as a time of getting acquainted.

It will be valuable to have at hand at least one copy of *COVENANTING TOWARD UNITY: From Consensus to Communion*; this text describes the larger context of actions that the Consultation is proposing, of which claiming the CONSENSUS is one element. This larger context is called "covenanting."

It is also desirable that each of the sessions should conclude with worship, perhaps of various styles and traditions, especially if persons from several different communions are present. It is suggested that the final worship be a celebration of Holy Communion, utilizing the COCU service "Sacrament of the Lord's Supper — A New Text."

The basic question to be addressed at the close of the study is this: Can we, members of the same churches which gathered at the 1984 Plenary meeting of COCU, now affirm, accept, and claim THE COCU CONSENSUS as a sufficient theological basis for moving ahead in the quest of a united and uniting church?

Gerald F. Moede
General Secretary

SESSION I: Getting Started

Purpose: To get to know the members of the group and some basic background information about the Consultation on Church Union.

The group should begin with introductions, including church membership and perhaps the "faith background" of each person, so that the varieties of ways in which the Spirit touches lives may become part of the group consciousness. Then ecumenical experiences can also be shared — worship, mission projects, "mixed-marriages" in a family, councils of churches, etc.

We suggest in this first session that the group view the 24-minute videotape introducing COCU entitled "That the World May Believe." (See list of Basic Resource Materials.) This tape gives a brief historical background of the COCU effort in recent years, and puts the Consultation into its current context. At the conclusion of the videotape, the leader might ask group members to reflect together upon what they learned about COCU from the video, and what they feel about this ecumenical venture.

The remainder of the first session can be spent in distributing copies of the CONSENSUS document, and reading through the Table of Contents and Foreword. Of crucial importance is understanding the questions being asked of each church (page 2). These questions need to be in the minds of the group members throughout the sessions; they form the underlying basis of what the Consultation has tried to do in this theological text.

SESSION 2: Understanding the Basics

Purpose: To examine the nature of the unity we seek — not a merger, but a diversity-in-communion.

By the second session, each participant should have read THE COCU CONSENSUS. Make sure that the three questions to be asked to each church (page 2 of the Foreword) have been read and grasped, so that each person understands the purpose of the consensus statement. At the same time, reference should be made to what is meant by "claiming" this consensus document (see pages 2-3, Foreword). Note that the CONSENSUS is said to be "an expression of" the faith we hold in common — "to claim it" means to recognize in it an expression of the faith of the Church sufficient to make next steps in covenanting possible. It does *not* mean seeing in the document "complete unanimity or uniformity of expression" by any particular communion. Nor does it imply that any of the churches will agree totally with the forms of expressing the faith of the Church contained in this document.

Ask the group to discuss the four points identified on page 3 of the Foreword.

Chapter I: Why Unity?

Why are we seeking unity? Even after twenty-five years together in the Consultation, this question still needs to be addressed. Chapter I of the CONSENSUS details many of the major reasons for working toward visible unity. Yet, there still remain those who say, "We already have spiritual unity and that's enough."

Discuss briefly the many biblical texts cited (paragraphs 4-6). In what way does Christian division hamper true witness and evangelism? How do racism, sexism, or discrimination against persons with disabilities divide the Church of Christ (paragraphs 15-17)?

Chapter II: Unity: A Gift to be Made Visible

What kind of unity are we seeking? The next step of unity COCU envisages is not yet organic union, but it is a far more united style of life and mission than now exists. Although some persist in thinking of the Church of Christ Uniting as a kind of "merger," it is anything but that. Rather, what is intended is more a process of growing together in which each communion will respect and come to appreciate the traditions of the other, in which each will recognize the other, and share with the other. The institutional expression of that union is still unknown.

Chapter II suggests that the unity we seek needs to be made visible, that celebration of God's grace will be central, that Christ's ongoing mission of salvation for the entire world will mark every endeavor of this pilgrimage, that the structures of the uniting effort will mirror the diversity of its present members, and that previous ecumenical relationships of each communion will be maintained and strengthened. And, it is hoped that renewal and reformation will characterize the entire effort in pursuing a unity-with-diversity and diversity-in-communion.

Questions: How do you respond to the seven distinctive characteristics that should mark the life of the uniting church of the future? Is the open-ended nature of this undertaking made clear enough? This chapter tries to suggest that the diversity that characterized the early Church may validly exist to enrich the kind of church life we seek together. Is this point made forcefully enough?

SESSION 3: Fundamental Understandings of Church and Membership

Purpose: *To understand the calling of the Church to be catholic, evangelical, and reformed, and the meaning of church membership in a uniting church.*

The background for this session is Chapters III and IV. Covering this material in one session will be very difficult. It would help if someone in the group has studied each chapter intensively in advance, and will be prepared to summarize it.

Chapter III: Toward a Church Catholic, Evangelical, and Reformed

Each of the churches in the Consultation tends to understand its background by stressing one or another of these perspectives on the church's life and witness. Is each word completely understood? Is it made clear that *each* of them needs to characterize a Church Uniting?

Catholic — means universal, all-inclusive, expressing the one faith received by the original apostles, and expressing in its life and worship that faith.

Questions: Where does our communion fall short of being "catholic?" Can we accept that word as being important, since one world-wide church already uses it in its name? What changes would be implied for us to be truly catholic?

Evangelical — stresses the preaching of the Good News of Christ by word and deed. It includes an acceptance of the authority of the Scripture, and lays stress also on the influence of the Holy Spirit.

Questions: Many of us have known a kind of "evangelicalism" that is inner-directed, narrow, and world-denying. What does "truly evangelical" imply for our faith and its witness in the world? How can a church be both "catholic" and "evangelical?"

Reformed — the Church is by its very nature a self-critical, continually evolving organism; if it becomes an uncritical, self-congratulatory arm of the society in which it finds itself, it is no longer true to its nature. God's judgment calls for continual reform — thus the Church Uniting needs to be a church *semper reformanda.*

Questions: Do we really believe that the household of God is the place where divine judgment begins (I Peter 4:17)? How do we maintain willingness and openness to be continually reformed?

Chapter IV: Membership

Certain basic points are made in this chapter. Membership in the Church is always membership in a particular local community. Membership is without regard to characteristics of race, sex, disability, or gifts. The marks that generally signify entrance into the Church are normally these:

- baptism with water in the name of the Father, Son, and Holy Spirit;
- public confession of faith;
- participation in the life of the Church – its worship, mission;
- participation in the life of the world, always acting in the light of the message of saving and sacrifice that comes through Christ. This signifies mutual love and suffering among members;
- membership involves growth, maturation, and discipline.

Questions: Each of the communions in the Consultation has accepted the membership of the others. What has this acceptance meant for the way they make decisions and live their lives? What does it mean for our understanding of baptism as the primary act of initiation into the life and membership of the church? (Some of the COCU member churches already invite persons from other denominations to serve in their legislative assemblies with full voice and vote.) How do we care for the growth of our members in the faith throughout their lives, whether they were baptized as infants or adults (paragraphs 12, 13)? What would a church need to do in order that it may exercise discipline in love (paragraph 14)?

SESSION 4: Faith and Worship

Purpose: *To explore the interrelation of confessing the faith and common worship as essential elements in manifesting unity.*

Chapter V: Confessing the Faith

One of the primary theological breakthroughs of the ecumenical movement in recent years is a renewed understanding of the relationship between Scripture and Tradition. The essence of this relationship is described in paragraphs 4-7. Scripture and Tradition (with a capital "T") are not set over against each other. Rather, by *Tradition* is meant "the whole life of the Church insofar as, grounded in the life of Christ and nourished by the Holy Spirit, it manifests, confesses, and testifies to the truth of the Gospel." And, "in the Church, Scripture and Tradition belong together, since each is a manifestation, by and for faith, of the reality of Christ."

This chapter also describes the need for fresh confessions of faith, and for new understandings in how worship, mission, and inclusiveness all serve as "confession" of the faith as well. Faith must result in doing — thus the Church confesses its faith in the kinds of things it does and the settings in which it chooses to do them.

The document states that the Apostles' and Nicene Creeds are "unique, ecumenical witnesses of Tradition to the revelation of God recorded in the Scripture." It says that, although conditioned by historical circumstance, "they have transcended such limitations by their continuing power to set forth the reality and mystery of God's reconciling work in Jesus Christ" (paragraph 8), and that the Church Uniting will use these creeds in worship as acts of praise and allegiance to the Triune God (paragraph 8). The Church Uniting will also honor confessions of faith that have been used in the various traditions represented in the COCU member communions. While recognizing "that individual belief must be responsive to the public confession of the church," the text affirms that "formal assent to a creed cannot substitute for personal commitment" (paragraph 10).

Questions: How does the description of the living relation between Scripture and Tradition move us beyond some of the divisive arguments of the past? Is the relation between corporate confession and individual commitment a satisfactory statement of these ways of witnessing to the faith?

Chapter VI: Worship

A major way in which the Church witnesses to its faith is in worship. Since we as Christians have been freely given faith in Christ and his life, death, and resurrection, we respond in worship. This worship will contain certain elements, though these may be combined in various ways. In a Church Uniting there will be diverse forms of worship.

This chapter focuses on the two sacraments: Baptism and the Lord's Supper. Baptism is seen as a corporate act of worship, incorporating the baptized into Christ's death and resurrection. Appropriately differing forms of baptism are to be maintained in a Church Uniting. A reaffirmation of baptismal vows is foreseen in confirmation, especially for those baptized in infancy.

The Lord's Supper is seen to be an act of congregational thanksgiving for the perfect sacrifice of Jesus Christ. His act of sacrifice gathers up our self-offering, and unites them with his own (paragraph 16). By reason of Christ's presence in the action, believers truly share the gifts and fellowship of his table. Further, "a Church Uniting will recognize and respect different views as to whether there are other ordinances which merit being called sacraments . . ." (paragraph 19).

Questions: Is the description of how both infant and believer's baptism emphasize different aspects of God's grace sufficient to hold both practices of baptism in the Church Uniting (paragraph 11)? Can churches which confirm those baptized in infancy agree to confirmation being part of a lifelong reaffirmation of baptismal vows (paragraph 14)? Most churches in the Consultation are moving to a more frequent celebration of the Lord's Supper. Paragraph 15 speaks of it as "standing at the heart of the Church's worship;" paragraph 17 says, "Christ in the Lord's Supper effectually shares with his People all that has been accomplished in his incarnation, atoning death, resurrection, and exaltation." Does this comprehensive statement encourage us to make this sacrament a more regular part of our worship life?

SESSION 5: Ministry

Purpose: *To examine the issues and challenges of achieving a mutual reconciliation of ministries, and to understand the ministries being proposed for a Church of Christ Uniting.*

Chapter VII: Ministry

The "Note on the Function of Chapter VII" at the beginning of this chapter describes its intention; it points out that what follows is a sketch of the shape of ministry in the Church Uniting — different from any now existing in the nine member communions.

At the outset we read that Christian ministry is the continuation of Christ's ministry (paragraph 27); all are given gifts and each has a ministry. Both lay and ordained ministries of the Church are differing forms of the one ministry of Christ that is shared by the whole People of God (paragraph 21). All ministry in the Church Uniting will be personal, collegial, and communal. Lay persons have a vital place in Christian ministry (paragraphs 24-26); indeed, lay status is the "primary form of ministry apart from which no other Christian ministry can be described" (paragraph 25). This ministry is that to which all are commissioned at baptism.

Regarding the ordained ministry, the document states, "Within the one ministry of the whole People, God calls forth in the Church particular ministries of persons to serve the People through proclamation of the Word and administration of the sacraments (paragraph 30). Ordination marks these persons as those "who represent to the Church its own identity and mission in Jesus Christ" (paragraph 31).

Although several orderings of ministry have existed in church history, the document advocates the threefold pattern of bishop, presbyter, and deacon as the most widely accepted through the history of the Church which provides a means to serve as an expression of the unity we seek. With continuing renewal, the threefold ordering will be developed in the Church Uniting in ways appropriate to the differing traditions of the uniting churches (paragraph 44).

The ministry of *bishop* is described as liturgical leader, teacher of the apostolic faith, pastoral overseer, leader in mission, representative minister in the act of ordination, administrative leader, servant of unity, and participant in governance. That of *presbyter* (priest, elder, pastor) is described as preacher of the Word, celebrant of the sacraments, teacher of the Gospel, pastoral administrator, leader in mission, servant of unity, and participant in governance. The ministry of *deacon* described here represents some new understandings of this office in the ordained ministry of the Church. The description is that of a renewed ministry of deacon which attempts to combine the traditional role of service both to Church and the world. The diaconal ministry is that which exemplifies the interdependence of worship and mission, Church and world.

Questions: What changes would the acceptance of this three-fold pattern mean for us in our present ministries of oversight? of presbyter? of deacon?

In thinking about the description of the "bishop" in this chapter it may be helpful to briefly consider that office or group in your church which most closely correspond with the ministry of bishop as described. It would also be fruitful for discussion groups to study the ministry of "deacon" outlined here to discover how this ministry might enhance and renew the life and witness of the Church in its service to Christ's mission.

* * * * * * * * * * * * * *

In a *concluding* period, ask the group to review its work and discussion over the past five sessions: what did they discover that was new and exciting? What did they discover which presents problems or concerns? Look again at the three questions in the resolution from the 16th Plenary addressed to the churches (page 2), and ask: Can *we* now claim this Consensus along the lines of the purposes offered in that resolution? What suggestions would we offer to the Consultation as it continues its work on behalf of its member churches in the quest for a Church of Christ Uniting?

[All groups are strongly urged to continue their use of the COCU process by turning to examine the proposals for the next steps in *COVENANTING TOWARD UNITY: From Consensus to Communion.*]

Worship: A celebration of the Lord's Supper using the COCU liturgy.

Basic Resource Materials

GENERAL

COCU Brochure: A brief informational brochure describing the present and hope of the Consultation. Bulk orders over 100: 5¢ each; available in large quantities.

Oneness in Christ: The Quest and the Questions; Traces COCU's life in the 1970s; discusses the primary ecumenical questions of the 1980s and COCU's relation to these questions; written by Gerald Moede. $4.50.

That the World May Believe; a 25-minute VHS video cassette on the life and future of the Consultation. Available for purchase for $30 from COCU, or can be rented for $10 from: Ecufilm; 810 Twelfth Avenue South, Nashville, Tennessee 37203; (800) 251-4091.

THEOLOGICAL

THE COCU CONSENSUS: In Quest of a Church of Christ Uniting; Twenty years in the making, this consensus statement is being sent to the churches for their reception; it forms the theological basis for covenanting. Available for $1.25 per copy, plus 69¢ postage. Discount for bulk orders.

COVENANTING RELATED

COVENANTING TOWARD UNITY: From Consensus to Communion; the covenanting proposals, and the liturgies for covenanting, being sent to the COCU member churches for study and response. Available at a cost of $1.00, plus 69¢ postage. Discount for bulk orders.

COCU and Covenant; Austin Seminary Bulletin. An entire issue of this seminary journal devoted to covenanting. Essays by F. Garcia-Treto, W. Eugene March, John F. Jansen, Robert S. Paul, Lewis S. Mudge, and Paul A. Crow, Jr. Can be ordered from COCU for $1 plus 69¢ postage.

Covenanting For Unity: A Next Step Forward? A study of covenants, both in biblical and recent church history. Projects covenanting as a possible way for the Consultation. Available from COCU for $1 plus 69¢ postage.

Consultation on Church Union
Research Park, 151 Wall Street
Princeton, NJ 08540

which was intended in creation, this community strives, by the fellowship of its members, to symbolize God's intention for all humanity (Jn. 3:16-17; Phil. 1:27).

9) The Church Uniting which we envision would accept as outward and visible bonds or marks of Church membership those confessions, attitudes, and acts which derive from the living traditions of the Church in all ages and places, and which are consistent with Scripture. Among such bonds or marks, normally present in unison, are the following:

[a] *Baptism with Water in the Name of Father, Son, and Holy Spirit* (Matt. 28:19). Baptism effects or signifies the union of the one baptized with Christ, and in Christ, with all members of his body, the universal Church. Thus our baptism is a basic bond of unity. Baptism in the case of adults is the enactment of a personal decision of faith, repentance, and loving obedience, which is a response in the power of the Spirit to the gracious call of God in Christ. In the case of infants it is the act by which the child of a Christian family is sacramentally placed within the sphere of God's grace and the Church's pastoral nurture, with a view to being taught and led to a subsequent act of personal faith in Christ (VI: 10-13).

[b] *Public Confession of Faith* (I Tim. 6:12; Rom. 10:9-10). Public confession of faith means the confession of Jesus Christ as Lord and Savior, of the One who raised him from the dead, and of the Spirit by which Christ dwells in our hearts. Normally it takes place in the presence of the congregation, either at the time of Baptism in the case of professing believers, or at the time of confirmation by those who were baptized as infants. Such confession, rooted in the experience of grace and repentance, involves deep and persistent commitment to learn the way of Christ while striving to walk within it (VI:4).

[c] *Faithful Participation in the Life of the Church* (Acts 2:42-47; I Cor. 16:1-3). Members participate in the life of the Church in the first instance through active sharing in worship both public and private, and in particular through faithful worship in the context of the Lord's Supper. They further participate in its life through study of Scripture and earnest thought concerning God's will for the world and the Church, and through the generous support of its life and mission by gifts, by work, and by active devotion.

[d] *Faithful Participation in the Life of the World*. Members of Christ's body bear witness, in action and speech, to God's presence in the world (Matt. 24:14; Jn. 8:12, 17:11, 14:21). This mission they carry out by the way in which they participate not only in affairs connected with their family and their job, but also in those of the community at large: politics, education, leisure, and art. By personal acts of service and sometimes resistance, which aim to actualize justice, mercy, and peace, and by active work to alter structures which deny God's will for humanity, they participate in the life of Christ.

The Development of Membership

10) Membership develops as people "grow up in every way into him who is the head, into Christ, from whom the whole body, joined and knit together by every joint with which it is supplied, when each part is working properly, makes bodily growth and upbuilds itself in love" (Eph. 4:15-16).

11) A person enters upon this membership through a many-sided sharing in the life of the Christian community, within which, as the gospel is heard and received in faith, he or she freely and personally appropriates the grace of Christ conveyed in Baptism. A person continues in this membership by continual sharing in the grace which creates and animates the Christian community. This involves participation in the preaching of the Word and the celebration of the sacraments. It involves learning and sharing a spirituality and a manner of life worthy of the gospel. It involves having an active part in the life of mutual concern and care which characterize brothers and sisters in Christ. It involves accepting the common Christian life of service, reconciliation, and witness. A person manifests this membership by allowing the Spirit of Christ to nurture and develop the talents and vocation which are the seeds of a unique individual life of ministry and witness to God (Rom. 6:3-13).

12) Christian nurture is fundamentally a sharing in the life of Jesus who says: "I am the vine, you are the branches. He who abides in me, and I in him, he it is that bears much fruit" (Jn. 15:5). It is thus the Church's provision for the growth of all its members in all aspects of Christian life, understanding, and witness, throughout their entire lives. It manifests an impulse which is inherent in Christian faith: to seek growth in knowledge, love, and discernment for the sake of maturity in Christ, a manner of life worthy of the gospel, and "a spirit of wisdom and revelation in the knowledge of him" (Eph. 1:17).

13) Christian nurture is also an indispensable instrument of the Church's mission. Children and other persons who look forward to confession of faith and church membership need instruction in the meaning of Christian faith and discipleship and in the challenge to commit their lives to Christ. Persons who are already members need continuing Christian education and training to develop the maturity, understandings and skills needed in the life of discipleship and witness. It is especially important in the present time that members learn how to develop and express their own contemporary interpretations of the Christian message and life, so that when called to do so, they "account for the hope that is in them" (I Pet. 3:15).

14) The recovery and clarification of Christian discipline — considered by our forebears in the faith to be a mark not only of the individual believer but of the Church — is an essential task as churches work towards union. A Church which knows that there is no discipleship apart from a disciplined life will be equipped to face the divisions and discriminations that too frequently infect Christian fellowship. Within the freedom of those who have been set free in Christ, the Church relies not so much on rules and

church laws as on the power of the gospel to shape communal and personal life and spirituality. Yet the Church must be prepared to root out barriers within its life due to race, sex, age, disability, and other such factors. Fundamentally, Christian discipline is also a sharing in the life of the Jesus who says: "As a branch cannot bear fruit by itself, unless it abides in the vine, neither can you, unless you abide in me." "Every branch of mine that bears no fruit, he takes away, and every branch that does bear fruit, he prunes, that it may bear more fruit" (Jn. 15:2). Such fruit — love, joy, peace, patience, kindness, goodness, faithfulness, gentleness, self-control (Gal. 5:22-23) — contributes to the credibility of the Church's witness. The discipline of Christ by which this fruit is cultivated is indispensable in the Church's ministry of shepherding, safeguarding as it does the apostolic message and worship, and guiding the life and witness of its members. Today, moreover, it is important to stress the corporateness of this ministry of discipline by encouraging the mutual care and concern of Church members (III:7,d).

15) As a cherished aspect of its internal diversity and thus as a contribution to the richness of its unity, the Church Uniting will recognize a call to certain of its members to associate together in special covenantal communities, sharing a common life under a rule of prayer, service, and growth. Undertaken in unity with the Church, the establishment and maintenance of such communities will be of great value to the whole Church's life, witness, and work.

Mutual Recognition of Members

16) Since all believers who are baptized into Jesus Christ are members of his body and share in his ministry, it is therefore appropriate that the covenanting churches have mutually recognized one another's members as sharing a common membership and ministry in the whole People of God (Acts 15:4; I Cor. 1:2; Rom. 15:25-27, 16:1-23).

V
Confessing The Faith

1) The Church lives and finds its identity in thankful confession of Jesus Christ as the one Lord and Savior (Col. 1:15-20). In Christ God's purpose for humanity is effectively made known (Eph. 1:9-10). Christ is God's self-giving in the Holy Spirit to be the life of the People of God (Jn. 1:4; Rom. 8:2). Christ therefore is "our wisdom, our righteousness and sanctification and redemption" (I Cor. 1:30). Being justified by faith in Christ, we are reconciled to God and to one another through the faith and love which is bestowed in the Spirit (II Cor. 5:18-19; I Cor. 13). The Church thus confesses and worships in glad celebration the one triune God (Matt. 28:19; II Cor. 13:14).

2) The content of the Church's confession is the apostolic preaching and faith which it continuously hears, believes, and expresses anew (I Cor. 15:1-15). This essential Tradition is handed on by being confessed not only in Scripture and creeds, but also in preaching and teaching, in forms of praise and prayer, and in witness and action obedient to the Lord.

3) The Church Uniting will acknowledge that the Head of the Body has made it a steward and trustee of this gospel (I Cor. 4:1). As it seeks to protect the integrity of the gospel, it will not merely preserve the common faith, but also will allow it to bear fruit in the personal commitment and action of individuals. It will seek the gospel's meaning not only in the witness of Scripture and Tradition but also in interpretations of faith made in the light of personal and communal experience and of careful reasoning. It will seek to grasp the fullness of the one Christ in and through the historical and cultural diversity of human expressions of the "grace and truth" which are his (Eph. 1:22-23).

Scripture

4) The source and basis of this faith and the confession of it is the creative and redemptive action of God in Christ, known through the prophetic and apostolic witness definitively borne in the Bible. The Church Uniting will therefore acknowledge the unique and normative authority of Holy Scripture. Scripture is the supreme rule of the Church's life, worship, teaching, and witness. It conveys all that is necessary for salvation to those who seek it in faith. The inspired testimony of Scripture belongs to the saving event by which God has, in Christ, constituted the Church and

promised his final reign (Lk. 4:17-21; II Tim. 3:16; I Cor. 4:6). The Holy Scripture is the norm of the Church's confession, and therefore of its identity. It is the source of new life and light as the Holy Spirit makes fruitful in the Christian community the Word of God (III:10,b).

5) The Word incarnate is Jesus Christ, the living Lord, the Head of the Church (Jn. 1:14). Christ is the truth which the community seeks and finds in the Holy Scriptures (Jn. 5:39; Lk. 24:27, 32). In Christ the promises of God are fulfilled; to Christ the Apostolic writings bear witness. Christ is the Word to whom the Scriptures and the Spirit testify (Acts 18:28; Jn. 16:13-15).

Tradition

6) There is an historic Christian Tradition to which every Christian body inevitably appeals in matters of faith and practice. In this Tradition three aspects can be distinguished, although they are inseparable. [a] By *"Tradition"* (with a capital "T") is meant the whole life of the Church insofar as, grounded in the life of Christ and nourished by the Holy Spirit, it manifests, confesses, and testifies to the truth of the gospel (I Jn. 1:1-4). This uniting Tradition comes to expression in teaching, worship, witness, sacraments, way of life, and order. [b] Tradition is also the *process of transmitting* by which this living reality of Christ is handed on from one generation to another. [c] And, since Tradition is this continually flexible and growing reality as it is reflected, known, and handed on in the teaching and practice of the Church, Tradition is also embodied and expressed more or less adequately in a variety of concrete historical *traditions* (lower case "t").

7) In the Church, Scripture and Tradition belong together, since each is a manifestation, by and for faith, of the reality of Christ. They are related in at least these ways. [a] Scripture is itself included in the Tradition. Christian Tradition, drawing on and in many ways continuous with the traditions of Israel, antedated the formation of the Church's biblical canon. [b] Scripture is the focal and definitive expression of the Tradition of the apostles. As such, it is the supreme norm and corrector of all traditions. The Church has acknowledged this by binding itself to the Scripture as its canon. The use of Scripture in worship and the authority of Scripture over the teaching of the Church are essentials in the life of the Christian community.

Creeds and Confessions of the Church

8) The Church Uniting will acknowledge the Apostles' Creed and the Nicene (Constantinopolitan) Creed as unique, ecumenical witnesses of Tradition to the revelation of God recorded in Scripture. These are ancient and widely accepted statements in which community and individual alike enact their identity by confessing their faith. Both of these creeds grew out of baptismal confessions of faith as the early Church struggled to test and clarify its understanding of the gospel, and have been used as short affirmations and summaries of the Church's witness and belief. Although

conditioned by the language and thought of their time, these symbols (creeds) have transcended such limitations by their continuing power to set forth the reality and mystery of God's reconciling work in Jesus Christ.

9) The Church Uniting will use these creeds in worship as acts of praise and allegiance to the Triune God, thus binding itself to the apostolic faith of the one Church in all centuries and continents (Acts 2:42). In its duties as a guardian of the truth of the gospel, the Church will teach the faith of these creeds, recognizing the historically conditioned character of their language, their corporate nature, and the principle that they are witnesses to and instruments of God's New Covenant with humanity in Christ (II Cor. 3:5-6).

10) The Church Uniting will acknowledge that every member has a direct relationship with God within the community of faith. It will, therefore, seek to respect the conscientious conviction of individual members and to enhance the deeply personal character of Christian faith. Only by the costly, individual choice and obedience which grace enables can a person trust in Jesus Christ and be fully committed to him. Corporate confessions are intended to guard, guide, and embody this personal commitment within the community. Although individual belief must be responsive to the public confession of the Church, formal assent to a creed cannot substitute for personal commitment (Matt. 15:1-3; Col. 2:8-10).

11) The Church Uniting will honor the distinctive understandings of the faith which God has historically committed to the uniting churches and which they have sought to express in formal confessions (Rom. 1:18; Col. 1:3-5; I Pet. 2:21-24; Eph. 4:4). Each of them has ordered its life under the authority of Scripture. Each has made its own the apostolic testimony to God's redemption. Each has responded in special ways to the truth of the gospel, and embodied the theological insight thus achieved in corporate covenants and confessions. The tradition represented by each of these will enrich corporate understanding of the gospel. In the diversity of its life, the Church Uniting has room for those confessions which are cherished by any of the covenanting bodies. It will value such confessions as they serve the renewal and revitalization of the Church in a common scriptural faith. It will not permit any such confession to become an exclusive requirement for all its members, or to become a basis for divisions within its community. As it grows in unity, it will outgrow or resolve such divisive disputes as are no longer compelling to faith or theology.

12) The responsibility of the Church Uniting as a guardian of the apostolic Tradition will include, as a part of its preaching and teaching office, an obligation to confess and communicate from time to time the substance of the faith in new language to meet new occasions and issues (II Cor. 3:4-6; I Pet. 3:15). In formulating such fresh confessions, it will work under the authority of the Scriptures, seeking the guidance of the Holy Spirit (I Jn. 4:1-2).

13) Faithful guardianship also entails an obligation to help the members of each covenanting church to rediscover a more comprehensive

tradition of covenants and confessions (Eph. 3:14-19). There are other churches, not represented in the Consultation, to whom we are bound in one Lord, one faith, one Baptism (Eph. 4:5). These churches have expressed their stewardship of the gospel in their own symbols and creeds. A Church Uniting will study these confessions, and where possible, join in them, thus enhancing the strength and richness of the common faith and expressing the fuller uniting of the Body of Christ.

Worship as Confession

14) Confession of faith takes place not only, or even primarily, in the setting forth of doctrinal confessions, but also in the forms and acts of common public worship (Jn. 4:22-24; Acts 2:46-47). The Church Uniting will therefore order its services of worship to express faith in Christ. By its celebration of the Word of God — through the reading of Scripture and the response of prayer and praise, through preaching and responsive hearing, through the ministry of the sacraments, and also through expression in music, architecture and other arts — it will confess Christ as the source and foundation of life.

Mission as Confession

15) Because it inherits the apostolic and evangelical calling, the Church Uniting will be summoned to exercise toward individual persons as well as society a mission which is both prophetic and reconciling (Acts 1:8; Rom. 1:5; Eph. 3:7-10; Lk. 4:18-21; 12:49-56; II Cor. 5:18-20). The carrying out of this calling is a further essential form of its confession of Christ. The Church will therefore seek continually to clarify its understanding of the eternal gospel, and to convey that understanding in its public appeal to the world. It will aim to set forth the essentials of Christian faith in terms intelligible to the people among whom it is called, without at the same time weakening the demands which follow from Christ's work as Judge and Redeemer of all (I Cor. 2:1-5). It will aim to address the contemporary issues of public life, knowing the conflict between "the wisdom of God" and "the wisdom of the world," and knowing also that Christ has reconciled the world to God (I Cor. 1:20-21).

16) Serving in Christ's name and following his example, the Church will seek to confess its faith by giving itself in suffering love for the world. By translation of faith into deeds in this way the Church can participate in the suffering and glory of the crucified and risen Lord (Col. 1:24). In each situation, while keeping open to new knowledge and sincere criticism by others, it will seek to bear witness to the presence of God, who rules and overrules in all human affairs and enterprises.

Inclusiveness as Confession

17) The Church knows and acknowledges that humanity is both diverse and one, because it confesses that in Jesus Christ all men and women are

offered redemption. Therefore, every person who confesses Christ as Lord is by that very confession bound to other persons as neighbors (I Jn. 4:11, 19-21). For this reason, the Church Uniting must not only call to mind the judgments of God upon the injustices and sins of the past, but also address itself to contemporary wrongs which alienate people from themselves, from their neighbors, from the created order of which they are a part, and from God.

18) To be faithful to its confession of faith, therefore, the Church must stand against all forms of prejudice, hatred, false nationalism, or discrimination based upon supposed social, racial, mental, physical, or sexual superiority. The Church Uniting will confess that such discrimination denies the unity of the God whose love is the same for all human beings, obscures the truth of one Lord and one humanity, and degrades the oppressor even while it inflicts injustice upon the oppressed (Matt. 22:37-40; Eph. 1:9-10; James 2:1-7; Acts 17:24-28; Gal. 3:28). Congregations, individuals, or groups of Christians who exclude, exploit, or patronize any of their sisters or brothers, however subtly, offend God and place the profession of their faith in doubt (III:7,b).

19) The Church Uniting will affirm the diversity, equality, and dignity of all persons. It will identify itself with those for whom justice has been thwarted, and will support them in their struggle (Matt. 25:31-46; James 2:15-17). Rectification of past inequities is urgently needed. Thus the Church Uniting will insist upon freedom from discrimination due to race, sex, age, class, physical or mental condition within its own life, and will work for the abolition of injustice in society at large. In this effort to express the love of God for all people and to eliminate the idolatry which is implicit in every kind of human discrimination, the educational program of the Church Uniting will stress continually the inclusiveness of the People of God, as that is given in the Christ whom it confesses as Lord.

VI
Worship

The Meaning of Worship

1) The essence of worship is a response of thanksgiving for God's holy love revealed supremely in Jesus Christ (Phil. 4:6-7; I Cor. 11:24). Through worship we are enabled to join those who in all times and places have offered the sacrifice of praise and obedience to God through "Christ Jesus, who died, yes, who was raised from the dead, who is at the right hand of God, who indeed intercedes for us" (Rom. 8:34).

2) It is Christ who has made this sacrifice on our behalf (Heb. 9:24-26). We are joined to Christ in our worship by the renewing power of the Holy Spirit, through whom we are enabled to offer the response of praise for which the universe and humanity were created (Rom. 8:26-27, 19-23). Since the God who creates and saves also governs according to his own purpose, the worship of the Church is an act of confident hope that the kingdom shall come and God's will be done on earth as it is in heaven (Matt. 6:10).

Forms of Worship

3) Corporate worship centers in the proclamation of the Word and the celebration of the sacraments. The individual believer's prayer, obedience, and service are essential components of the entire community's worship.

4) The public worship of the Church is an act by which the Church offers itself to God (I Pet. 2:5). It includes corporate acts of praise, confession of sin, thanksgiving and prayer, the reading and hearing the Scriptures, the preaching and hearing the Word of God, affirmation of faith, and the celebrating of the sacraments. Because public worship is an act of the entire People of God, it involves the lively participation of all members, not only in hymns and prayers but also in the acts of preaching and hearing, and in sacramental worship as corporate celebrants and communicants (Acts 2:42-47; I Tim. 2:1).

5) Forms of worship are important in the life of the Church for several reasons. They guard and transmit the Church's faith and witness; they foster the unity of God's people in its diversity; and they enable the familiar participation of all in public worship. As churches unite, new forms will be encouraged and old forms both used and cherished, or revised as seems wise. A variety of forms — especially as regards matters of ceremony,

church furnishings, vesture, music, and the like — is both natural and valuable. Forms of worship must be in accord with scriptural standards, which govern every expression of the Church's life and witness.

Corporate Worship

6) The Word of God, made flesh in Jesus Christ our Savior, is attested in the Scriptures of the Old and New Testaments (Jn. 1:14; 5:39, 46). It is the right and duty of believers to hear the full testimony of this prophetic and apostolic witness publicly and clearly read, and to bear witness in their own right to the truth and power of the apostles' message (I Tim. 4:13).

7) The apostolic message realizes its inherent aim only when it is interpreted, proclaimed, and applied in the present. In this way it awakens the faith and witness which constitute the living Church. Through preaching, the Word evokes hearing, repentance, faith, love, and witness. Such hearing, active as well as receptive, is an essential congregational contribution to corporate worship under the Word of God (Rom. 10:14-15; I Jn. 1:1-3; Matt. 13:23).

8) Congregational worship in which the preaching of the Word is conjoined with the celebration of the Lord's Supper is the constitutive and representative service of the community of apostolic faith (I Cor. 11:23-26; Acts 2:42). A sacrament is an effective sign and seal of the grace of God which is in Christ (Rom. 4:11; I Cor. 11:26). That is, it not only signifies God's redemption of humanity in Christ, but also, by God's faithful gift through the Spirit, it conveys that which it signifies as this is appropriated in the response of faith (Gal. 5:22-26; Acts 2:38). Christ may be called the fundamental sacrament of God's gracious encounter with humankind (Rom. 6:3-11; I Cor. 11:23-26).

9) The Church, then, as the body of Christ, may be seen as a sacrament of the Kingdom of God, appropriating its identity in Christ through faithful celebration of its most characteristic sacramental actions: Baptism and the Eucharist. The Church recognizes the central importance of the sacraments of Baptism and Holy Communion, which derive their authority from Christ as witnessed by the Scriptures (Matt. 28:19-20; I Cor. 11:23-26), and are integrally related to the founding events of the Christian community.

The Sacrament of Baptism

10) As an act of Christ and a proclamation of the gospel, Baptism is not a private affair but a corporate act of worship (Gal. 3:27-29). The act of Baptism effects, or signifies, the incorporation of the baptized into Christ's death and resurrection (Rom. 6:3-11; Col. 2:11-15), makes them living members of the Church universal (I Cor. 12:13), and by the power of the Holy Spirit enables them to confess their faith, to renounce sin and overcome death (Acts 2:38; Rom. 6:8), and in their new identity to commit themselves in a new life and ministry of love and righteousness, which are a foretaste here and now of the life of the Kingdom (Eph. 1:13-14). Baptism

as symbol, ordinance, and sacrament is a divine mystery and forms the visible basis of our unity in Jesus Christ. In Baptism all persons are made one in Christ Jesus. Human distinctions of race, class, gender, and physical and mental conditions are overcome (IV:9,a).

11) Scripture and Tradition are united in their witness that there is one Baptism (Eph. 4:5). Diversity of baptismal practice in the churches reflects different dimensions of the meaning of Baptism into the body of the one Lord. It is therefore appropriate that alternative practices be maintained within a Church Uniting. Infant Baptism calls attention to human need and helplessness, and to the reality of God's gracious initiative and action on our behalf. Baptism of confessing believers emphasizes the personal response to grace and the forgiveness of sin. It bears witness to the Church as a community reborn in the Spirit. Both infants and adults need responsible sponsorship by church members and adequate provision for Christian nurture.

12) Following instruction, Baptism is administered with water (by immersion, pouring, or sprinkling) in the name of the Father, the Son, and the Holy Spirit (Matt. 28:19,20; Jn. 3:5; Eph. 5:26). The rite includes an act of repentance on the part of the persons, or their sponsors; a confession of faith in God the Creator, in Jesus Christ and in the Holy Spirit; and a commitment by the person baptized or their sponsors, to a continuing life of obedience to Christ in the fellowship of the Church. Baptism is administered only once, normally by a presbyter with the participation of the sponsoring congregation.

13) The new life of membership in Christ and his Church must be continually and responsibly reaffirmed by the baptized persons so that they may fulfill the responsibilities of being called in Christ as ministers and witnesses in the world (Rom. 6:4, 12-14).

14) This lifelong reaffirmation of baptismal vows may include an act of worship, which at times has been called confirmation, consisting of prayer and the laying on of hands of those having been baptized as infants. Confirmation may also be understood as an effective sign of the continuing and growing incorporation into the life of Christ (Eph. 4:13-16), of which Baptism is the foundation and the Eucharist is the regular renewal. Baptism and confirmation signify both membership in the body of Christ and entrance into the ministry of the whole People of God (VII: 29).

The Lord's Supper

15) The sacrament of the Lord's Supper proclaims and recalls the life, death and resurrection of Christ while looking forward to Christ's return (I Cor. 11:23-26). In so doing it actualizes the unity and mission of the redeemed community, and thus, understood as including the preaching of the Word, it stands at the heart of the Church's worship (I Cor. 10:16-17; Acts 2:42, 20:7).

16) The liturgy of the Holy Communion is an act of congregational thanksgiving for the perfect sacrifice of Jesus Christ (Matt. 26:27; Heb.

9:24-26). By reason of his real presence in the action, believers truly share the gifts and fellowship of his table (Mk. 14:22-24; I Cor. 11:24-25). Christ's high priestly act of sacrifice gathers up our self-offerings of praise, thanksgiving, and service, and unites them with his own (Heb. 10:19-25). In this way the Church's work of prayer and service in the world anticipates the fulfillment of God's ultimate purpose "to unite all things in him, things in heaven and things on earth" (Eph. 1:10).

17) Thus Christ in the Lord's Supper effectually shares with his People all that has been accomplished in his incarnation, atoning death, resurrection, and exaltation. "The cup of blessing which we bless, is it not a participation in the blood of Christ? The bread which we break, is it not a participation in the body of Christ?" (I Cor. 10:16) God renews us corporately and individually in the life of the Spirit, and creates with us before the whole creation a visible and effectual sign of the reconciliation and liberation provided for humankind (Lk. 4:18-19; Eph. 1:13-14; II Cor. 5:16-21). Because Jesus Christ is its host and embodies the whole gospel, the Lord's Supper, wherever it is celebrated, is the communion of the universal Church of God (I Cor. 10:16-17).

18) In the celebration of the Eucharist the bread and cup are taken, they are blessed as thanks is given over them for God's creation and redemption of the world in Christ, the bread is broken, and the elements are shared among the congregation. The act of giving thanks includes recitation of Christ's Words of Institution as well as prayer invoking the Holy Spirit. The action is presided over by a bishop or presbyter, and deacons and lay persons assist in appropriate ways.

19) All of life, indeed, may be understood as invested with a certain sacramental quality through the activity of the creative and redemptive Word incarnate in Jesus Christ by the power of the Holy Spirit (Col. 1:15-20). A Church Uniting will recognize and respect different views as to whether there are other ordinances which merit to be called sacraments in the strict sense, such as confirmation, marriage, ordination, declaration of the forgiveness of sins, and anointing of the sick. The Church Uniting will recognize a sacramental quality in the Word of God preached, heard, or expressed through the visual arts, footwashing, feeding the hungry, giving of drink to the thirsty, welcoming the stranger, clothing the naked, and visiting the sick and the imprisoned.

VII
Ministry

A Note on the Function of Chapter VII in the Covenanting Process

The covenanting process proposed by the Church Order Commission of COCU and outlined in the *Foreword* to this Consensus document offers the participating churches a way to grow together toward a renewed and reconciled ministry. The shape of that new ministry, as envisioned by the Theology Commission, is sketched in the pages that follow. This sketch points toward an ordering of ministry which may well be different from that now found in any of the participating church bodies. But the indications offered here do not amount to a constitution. Many details are deliberately left unsettled. There is room for the participating churches to grow together in unforeseen ways as they work out the implications of the covenant.

The Theology Commission assumes that the ordering of ministry outlined in this chapter will first begin to appear concretely in the Councils of Oversight. (For more details see the Report of the Church Order Commission.) These bodies will be the initial bridges thrown across the chasms that now separate the churches from each other. As the covenanting churches give the Councils additional responsibilities, the provisions of this chapter will begin to be embodied in more detail. The details will also be modified in the light of experience, new insights, and the decisions made by the churches in their relations to each other.

In preparation for covenanting, and through the period of growing together in covenant, each church will be responsible for the enabling actions needed to permit it to designate representatives to the Councils of Oversight. Whatever offices these representatives may hold in their own churches, within the Councils they will be laypersons, deacons, presbyters, and bishops. The different nomenclatures and understandings concerning these ministries in the various churches will at the same time continue to exist. The old and the new orderings of ministry will thus exist side by side, informing and deepening each other. Certain polity changes in the participating churches may be needed to make this possible, but churches will make such changes only when they are ready to do so according to their own procedures. The anomalies in this situation will be frankly acknowledged. They will be minor in comparison to the anomaly of division itself.

The Consultation accordingly has not attempted to say in this chapter where any particular ministerial office of any particular church finds its place. The Consultation assumes that each covenanting body will decide where in its own polity to find persons whose ministries correspond to those represented in the Councils of Oversight.

The Ministry of Jesus Christ and the
Ministry of God's People

1) The life, death, and resurrection of Jesus Christ was a ministry of God to all humankind. Through the Holy Spirit, God's People are called to share that ministry and are empowered to fulfill what it requires. By the power of the same Spirit, the ministry of God's People appropriates and continues what God sent Jesus to be and do.

2) The ministry of Jesus Christ summed up and brought to focus all that God has done in the history of Israel and of all peoples to set men and women free and to reconcile them to one another and to God. His was therefore a liberating and reconciling ministry.

3) Sent by God to be and proclaim the fulfillment of all things in God's kingdom, Jesus Christ spoke with the authority of the Servant of God and humanity. Accordingly, Christ's mission was to preach good news to the poor, to proclaim release to the captives and recovering of sight to the blind, to set at liberty those who are oppressed, to proclaim the acceptable year of the Lord (Lk. 4:18; Isaiah 61:1). In Christ God began to put down the mighty from their thrones, and exalt those of low degree, to scatter the proud in the imagination of their hearts, to fill the hungry with good things and to send the rich empty away (Lk. 1:51-53).

4) Christ's authority was displayed in his healing the sick, forgiving sins, comforting the afflicted, challenging the arrogant, transforming traditions, and bringing into being a new covenant People in the midst of the old. Christ's authority was also made manifest in his announcement of the end of oppression and of the overturning of unjust power structures through the assertion of God's rule.

5) In solidarity with the outcast, and also with compassion for those who oppressed and executed him, Jesus Christ called all humankind to conversion and to repentance and summoned all to glorify God and love one another. The ministry of the risen Christ continues both through the life of the Church and through the intercessory role he now exercises in the presence of God.

6) Christ's ministry was also a reconciling ministry. In Christ, God was reconciling the world to God, not counting (our) trespasses against (us). For the sake of the human race God made Christ, who knew no sin, to *be* sin, so that in Christ we might become the righteousness of God (II Cor. 5:21). Therefore if anyone is in Christ, that person is a new creation (II Cor. 5:17).

7) God showed self-giving love for us, sending Christ to die for human sin (Rom. 5:8). We are justified by faith. As justified sinners we have peace

with God through Christ and his sacrifice on the cross (Rom. 5:1).

8) All this is from God, who through Christ reconciled us to God and gave us the ministry of reconciliation. Through Christ we have obtained access to God's grace in which we stand, and we rejoice in our hope of sharing the glory of God (Rom. 5:2).

9) Answering Christ's gracious summons, Christians by the Spirit are gathered into a ministering community, held together and empowered for service in love, hope, and faith.

10) In Christ, this People's life is vulnerable to suffering, yet strong in the midst of wickedness. This life offers and requires relationships of mutuality in need and service, and overcomes despair in the power of hope. This ministry is not confined to those of any one social or ethnic group. It is for and with the whole of humanity. Whenever obedience to Jesus Christ calls God's People to be in the world as he was in the world, they are led further by the Spirit into the truth of the gospel.

11) Enabled by grace, the People of God enters upon ministry by taking its stand where Christ is at work in the midst of humanity, in a continuing struggle against the powers of this age.

12) This struggle leads to both suffering and joy. Christ's People complete what is lacking of Christ's afflictions for the sake of his body, that is, the Church (Col. 1:24). They also know a foretaste of the joy that was set before him who endured the cross and is set down at the right hand of the throne of God (Heb. 12:2).

13) Therefore, where women and men struggle against poverty and oppression, ministry means entering into that struggle with oppressor and oppressed alike to overcome the causes of suffering. When men and women engage wittingly or unwittingly in oppressive actions and decisions, ministry means acting compassionately toward them for the eradication of these evils. Where people undergo affliction, pain, disease, and death, ministry means sharing witness with them in the calling to bear one anothers' burdens (Gal. 6:2). Where persons suffer because of their choice to work for liberation, justice, and peace, ministry means supporting them in their witness (Phil. 1:29, 30; Matt. 25:31-45).

14) Yet, ministry is not simply to those who suffer and struggle. All who struggle and suffer with hope minister to the world and offer compelling testimony to the power of the cross and resurrection. Such ministries may express to the Church the privilege of "dying daily" with Christ, and at the same time of rising with Christ to new life. For the ministry of God's People is at the same time joyful. Those who minister in the midst of suffering are called "blessed" (Matt. 5:1-11). They begin to inherit now a kingdom prepared for them before the foundations of the earth (Matt. 25:34). They are offered a foretaste of that messianic banquet at which the poor, the maimed, the blind, and the lame, have the privileged place (Lk. 14:13-14).

15) In all its forms and functions, ministry is a rich interweaving of word and worship, work and witness. In different ways, members of the body share responsibility for the Church's government, administration, discipline, instruction, worship, and pastoral care.

16) These activities are to be held together in a visible ordering through which the Church is equipped for its ministry. "Having gifts that differ according to the grace given to us" (Rom. 12:6), the several members bring to the one body a wide diversity of gifts, functions, and services. "To each is given the manifestation of the Spirit for the common good" (I Cor. 12:7). Each is a distinctive form of the single ministry of Christ as it is realized in diverse yet mutually complementary ways in the whole life of the Church and in the world (II:6,d; III:7,b; IV:3).

17) As the People gather to worship under the direction of the Word, all members both receive God's grace and make their contribution to the continuation of Christ's ministry before God.

18) There is a ministry of faithful hearing and proclaiming God's Word, of rightly administering and receiving the sacraments, of responsibly celebrating and living out the Church's worship. These are actions of the entire People of God. All members, including those with physical or mental impairments, are endowed with special gifts and vocations, and exercise particular functions, thus adding to the richness of Christ's ministry as it takes form in the worship of the gathered community.

19) Members of the Church are also called to labor as a People whose action manifests the ministry of Christ in the world. God's People bear witness to the world in and through the organized life of the Church (II: 7-8; III: 11). They are also summoned to be faithful witnesses in daily life: in trades, industry, agriculture, and commerce; in political life, education, and the family; in professional activity of every kind. They are summoned to forward God's redemptive ministry to humanity, to share in the ministry as a "living sacrifice" (Rom. 12:1), and to "prove what is the will of God" through the "renewal of (our) minds" on the way toward "what is good and acceptable and perfect" (Rom. 12:2).

20) The ministry of Jesus Christ, and the ministry of the Church in him, are intelligible only in relationship to God. In ministry the People enter into a cycle of life in the Spirit that leads from God and to God. Through the ministry of Christ and of his People, God's purpose of uniting all things in heaven and earth is being accomplished (Eph. 1:10).

The Sharing and Ordering of Ministry

21) The ordained and lay ministries of the Church are differing forms of the one ministry of Christ that is shared by the whole People of God. Because they are forms of one ministry, they complement one another. Thus, they must be ordered in relation to one another in the life of the Church.

22) All ministries, lay as well as those of bishop, presbyter, and deacon, are to be understood as at once personal, collegial, and communal. In attempting to actualize the personal, collegial, and communal character of ministry, the Church Uniting will seek to incorporate "catholic" and "protestant" concerns, as well as the experience of the different uniting

polities, drawing sustenance and admonition from the several converging streams of tradition.

[a] All ministry in the Church Uniting will be *personal*. In every minister, lay and ordained, Christ and the gospel are made present as personal reality and are the source of that life of holiness and devotion which is a mark of ministry. Ministry is exercised by men and women who have been individually called and baptized, and in certain cases, also ordained. They continue, in their activities, the ministry of Christ to the Church and to the world and, in turn, manifest the ministry of the Church to humanity. In their varying personal capacities, they serve individuals and groups within and outside the Church.

[b] All ministry in the Church Uniting will be *collegial*. Baptism and ordination alike associate the individual with others who share the same call. Ministry is inherently a shared responsibility. Thus no minister is independent or autonomous. Just as collegial relationships obtain among persons in the same ministry, so too they obtain among those in different ministries. Such relationships include lay persons as well as bishops, presbyters, and deacons. The interpersonal character of collegiality is a basis for partnership in governance and gives life and substance to the institutional structures of the Church.

[c] All ministry in the Church Uniting will be *communal*. The intimate relation between the different ministries and the Christian community as such should find expression in relationships through which the exercise of ministry is rooted in the life of the worshipping and witnessing congregation and requires the local church's effective participation in the discovery of God's will and the guidance of the Spirit.

23) All ministry in the Church Uniting will be constitutionally or canonically ordered and exercised in such a way that each of these three dimensions can find adequate expression. A person enters ministry through formal procedures of membership or ordination, accompanied by election or appointment. No individual's ministry can be regarded as representative of the Church unless it is constitutional or canonical, and remains in communion with and accountable to, other ministers in ordered assemblies in which all ministries are represented.

The Ministry of Lay Persons

24) Lay persons are called by their Baptism and membership in the Church to manifest and bear witness to Christ's presence in the world in all their activities. Through their Baptism, lay persons are called into the ministry of Jesus Christ, into a personal relationship to God in Christ, and at the same time into a relationship to other Christians. Lay persons who are subsequently ordained continue to bear responsibility for the ministry common to all Christians to which they were called at Baptism.

25) The terms "laity" and "laypersons" continually give rise to confusion, in part because of their apparent connection with *laos* or people,

a term applicable to the entire body of the Church, whether "lay" or "ordained." The derivation of the term "lay" is from the Greek *laos* or *laikos*, meaning "the people" or "of the people." But in common English usage the term "lay" means either "not ordained," or "not professional," and hence carries with it not only an inherent equivocation about the status to which it is the antonym, but also the suggestion of a deprived or residual character in the status to which it refers. In the list of Christian ministries, the "layperson" may thus be perceived as "none of the above," as one who does *not* have the duties or prerogatives of ordained persons. We wish to overcome this implication. Lay status in the Church is not a residual status, but rather the primary form of ministry apart from which no other Christian ministry can be described.

26) The ministry received in Baptism is at once personal, collegial, communal, and therefore also constitutional. Lay persons may be formally appointed to various functions, thereby being acknowledged by the Church, and, in turn, acknowledging their responsibility for particular tasks. They carry out their ministries in a variety of ways.

[a] *Witnessing to the Gospel in Worship and in the World.* Lay persons hear the gospel and proclaim it. They participate in the worship of the community by offering words and actions of praise, by taking part in the preaching whether by speaking or by responding, by reading the Scriptures, offering prayers, and bringing the eucharistic gifts. They fill lay offices in the congregation. They participate in educational programs, pursue private study, teach and bear witness to others. They inform and test current theological understandings. They discern and practice the implications of the gospel by word and action in their families, in the congregation, and in all places of daily living. In evangelism, they share their faith in Christ with others.

[b] *Seeking Justice and Reconciliation in the World.* Through active involvement in the world, lay persons represent Christ's ministry of justice and reconciliation. As agents of God's purpose, they speak from within the world to the world for a society both just and humane, where the needs of "the least" are met with sensitivity and dignity. They seek to discern the signs of the Kingdom wherever they may be manifest in human affairs as they bear witness to the gospel with boldness, courage, hospitality, and love.

[c] *Bringing the World before God.* The laity makes the connections between Christ, the Church, and the world real and visible. In their devotional practices and through their liturgical life, these persons offer to God their public and personal concerns and celebrate the mighty acts of God. By adoration, confession, thanksgiving, intercession, and supplication, they bring themselves and others under the transforming justice and mercy of God.

[d] *Providing Pastoral Care for Persons.* Lay persons are called to care for each other, for the ordained, and for persons outside the Church. Such caring means sensitive listening and discerning coun-

seling. It means visiting the sick, the prisoners, those confined by age
or poverty. It means participation in congregational and other
programs that enhance pastoral sensitivity to the hurts and dilemmas
faced by social groups, families, and individuals. It also means the
effort to address systemic social causes of human suffering.

[e] *Serving the Cause of Unity.* In virtue of their Baptism and
membership in the body, lay persons constitute an inherently
ecumenical ministry. In all they do, they embody this reality and raise
the question of unity for the Church Universal. Lay persons meet
across denominational lines in prayer and common mission. Thus
they can bring new expressions of the Church into being, acting out
forms of unity which the institutional churches cannot yet express.
They transcend divisions and express in anticipation the fulfilled
reality of the one body in Jesus Christ.

[f] *Participation in Governance.* Lay persons, bishops, presbyters, and deacons share in the governance of the Church locally,
regionally, and nationally.

The Ministry of Ordained Persons

27) The ministry of the one People of God, with all its diversity, is the
continuation of the saving ministry of Jesus Christ, and this ministry is the
context within which what is usually called ordained ministry must be
discussed.

28) According to growing ecumenical understanding, all members of
the Church are in a certain sense ordained to the whole, corporate ministry
(III:9): "As persons are initiated into the faith, they are, in a true sense,
ordained to a caring priesthood and to a company of witnesses to Christ"
(VI:14). The ministry is "a royal priesthood, a holy nation, a people for
God's own possession" (I Peter 2:9). Thus all Christians are called to
ministry, to a life of faithful discipleship in and beyond the Church. The
Church itself, indeed, was first known in New Testament Greek as *ek-
klesia*, having been called together from all peoples to be the People faithful
to God.

29) This calling of each Christian is sealed effectually by Baptism/
confirmation, when vows are taken and the responsibilities of discipleship
conferred. There are distinctions of function, but a shared dignity or worth
here, inasmuch as all are called to minister to one another and to all persons.

30) Within the one ministry of the whole People, God calls forth in the
Church particular ministries of persons to serve the People through
proclamation of the Word and administration of the sacraments (Lk. 22:
25-27; I Cor. 3:5; Acts 1:21-26, 6:1-6; II Tim. 1:11, 1:6). These ministries
share in the ministry of Christ by representing in and for the Church its
dependence on and its identity in, the Word of God (Jn. 20:21-23). For this
reason they symbolize and focus the ministry of Christ and the apostles as
well as the ministry of the whole Church. Those called to such public
ministries are ordained, in the *usual* sense of the term, by the Church

through the authority and power of the Holy Spirit (Acts 20:28). Minister, pastor, and preacher are general names for these persons; presbyter, priest, elder, deacon, and bishop are particular names.

31) These women and men share the whole ministry of witness and service with all the People of God. Their ordination marks them as persons who represent to the Church its own identity and mission in Jesus Christ. In this capacity they are authorized to undertake services in, with, and for the Church, preaching and teaching the gospel, presiding over the liturgical and sacramental life of the congregations, assembling, equipping, and watching over the community.

32) The authority of the ordained minister is rooted in Jesus Christ, who received it from God (Matt. 28:18) and who confers it by the Holy Spirit in the act of ordination. This act takes place within a community which accords public recognition to a particular person. Because Jesus came as one who serves (Mk. 10:45; Lk. 22:27), to be set apart means to be consecrated to service. Since ordination is essentially a setting apart with prayer for the gift of the Holy Spirit, the authority of the ordained ministry is not to be understood as the possession of the ordained person, but as a gift for the continuing edification of the body in and for which the minister has been ordained. (This paragraph is adapted from the WCC *Baptism, Eucharist and Ministry* document, Faith and Order Paper 111, 1982.)

33) Ordination is not to be confused with "professional" status within the Church. Some who are ordained will derive their salaries from the Church, while others will perform their ministries without leaving their occupation or employment. Requirements of education or specialized training will vary among participating churches and between the three offices. Regardless of these variations, ordination to the offices of deacon, presbyter, and bishop represents the call of God through the voice of the one Church rather than the "professional" achievement of a given individual.

34) People are called in differing ways. Sometimes persons are mistaken about the reality of their calling. From its beginnings however, the Church has recognized that several elements are essential in the call to the ordained, representative ministry. First, there is an inner, personal awareness and call, as the Holy Spirit bears witness to one's spirit (Rom. 8:16). Secondly, there is a recognition of the particular gifts and graces, both naturally and spiritually given, needed for ministry (Eph. 4:11). Thirdly, there is required the Church's public approbation that the call is an authentic call heard with good conscience. In the judgment of the Church, this call requires, for its fulfillment, possession and development of appropriate gifts for fruitful ministry.

35) The Church's act of ordination is performed in the name of Christ on the basis of God's call and gifts, which come without regard to disability, race, sex, mature age, social or economic status.

36) Those who are charged to make decisions about ordination, while seeking guidance of the Spirit, must rely on human wisdom and discretion. As fallible persons, they can err in accepting some and rejecting others, but faithfulness and serious purpose are presumed.

37) However the ordination ritual may be written or theologically interpreted, it consists essentially of prayer with the laying on of hands. (Proto-types of such practices in the New Testament are found, for example, in Acts 8:18, Hebrews 6:2, II Timothy 1:6.) The prayer is an invocation of the Holy Spirit, asking for divine power to be bestowed on the candidate for the exercise of this ministry. Believing that the prayer will be answered, as representatives of the whole Church, bishops and other persons place their hands upon the head of the ordinand, making a visible and effective sign of the gift of the Spirit, attesting the Church's approbation, and commissioning this person to fulfill a particular ministry. In recognition of the God-given nature of ministry, ordination to any one of the representative ministries is never repeated, just as Baptism is never repeated.

38) By the act of ordination the community of faith thankfully acknowledges that God provides women and men equipped with gifts and graces to lead and care for the Church in its total mission. By this act the minister, whether bishop, presbyter, or deacon, who shares with all members in the dignity of the priesthood of all believers, acknowledges an obligation to be a servant of God's servants, to the church bodies which ordain, to the Church Universal, and to Jesus Christ, the head of the Church.

The Threefold Pattern of Ordained Ministry

39) Several orderings of ordained ministry have arisen in the history of the Church. The exclusive warrant of the New Testament cannot be claimed for any one of them. They are adaptations of biblical forms to the needs of the Church in differing times and places. In the midst of this variety however, one ordering has emerged as predominant: the threefold ministry of bishop, presbyter, and deacon.

40) It is important to be aware of the changes the threefold ministry has undergone in the history of the Church. In the earliest instances, where threefold ministry is mentioned, the reference is to the local eucharistic community. The bishop was the leader of the community, was ordained and installed to proclaim the Word and preside over the celebration of the Eucharist. The bishop was surrounded by a college of presbyters and by deacons who assisted in his tasks. In this context, the bishop's ministry was a focus of unity within the whole community.

41) Soon, however, episcopal functions were modified. Bishops began increasingly to exercise oversight over several local communities at the same time in a manner analogous to the way the apostles had exercised oversight in the wider Church. Bishops thus began to provide a focus for unity in life and witness within areas comprising several eucharistic communities. As a consequence, presbyters and deacons were assigned new roles. Presbyters became the leaders of local eucharistic communities, and, as assistants of the bishops, deacons received larger responsibilities.

42) Although there is no single New Testament pattern, although the

Spirit has many times led the Church to adapt ministries to its contextual needs, and although other forms of the ordained ministry have been blessed with the gifts of the Holy Spirit, the threefold ministry of bishop, presbyter, and deacon may nevertheless serve today as an expression of the unity we seek and as a means for achieving it. Historically, the threefold ministry became the generally accepted pattern, and is still retained, in a variety of forms, by many churches today. Whatever nomenclature they may use, the churches need persons who in different ways express and perform the tasks of ordained ministry in its diaconal, presbyteral, and episcopal aspects and functions.

43) Yet the threefold pattern stands evidently in need of reform. In some churches the collegial dimension of leadership in the eucharistic community has suffered diminution. In others, the function of deacons has been reduced to an assisting role in the celebration of the liturgy: they have ceased to fulfill any function with regard to the diaconal witness of the Church. The relation of the presbyterate to the episcopal ministry has been discussed throughout the centuries. The degree of the presbyter's participation in the episcopal ministry is still for many an unresolved question of far-reaching ecumenical importance. In some cases, churches which have not formally kept the threefold form have, in fact, maintained certain of its original patterns.

(The five paragraphs above are adapted from the *Baptism, Eucharist, and Ministry* document, Faith and Order Paper 111, World Council of Churches, Geneva, 1982.)

44) In full awareness of these facts and of a continuing need for thoughtful attention to them, the threefold ordering will be continued in the Church Uniting in ways appropriate to the differing traditions of the uniting churches and to the future needs of their common mission. The ministry of the Church Uniting will be intended to manifest visible historical continuity "with the whole Christian fellowship in all places and in all ages in such wise that ministry and members are accepted by all" (WCC *New Delhi Statement*, 1961).

The Ministry of Bishops

45) Bishops are baptized members of the People of God, ordained to preach the Word, preside at the sacraments, and administer discipline in such a way as to be representative pastoral ministers of oversight, unity, and continuity in the Church.

46) Bishops, in communion with all the People of God, represent the continuity of the Church's life and ministry over the centuries, the unity of its communities and congregations with one another, and the oneness of its ministries in mission to the world. Bishops are a sign of, and are particularly responsible for, the continuity of the whole Church's Tradition (V:6), as well as of its pastoral oversight (in the Greek of the New Testament, *episkopé*), as they teach the apostolic faith.

47) Some churches have maintained episcopacy in the form of a succession of ordained ministers who combine in their ministries the

functions of both bishop and presbyter. Some other churches do not claim a formal episcopal succession, but in fact exist with the express intention of maintaining a succession in the apostolic faith. It is the intent of the participating churches that the apostolic content of such ministries, as well as the existence in them of ministries of *episkopé* in various forms, be fully recognized.

48) The participating churches intend that in the Church Uniting, bishops shall stand in continuity with the historic ministry of bishops as that ministry has been maintained through the ages, and will ordain its bishops in such a way that recognition of this ministry is invited from all parts of the universal Church.

49) In doing so, the Church Uniting will not require any theory or doctrine of episcopacy or episcopal succession which goes beyond the consensus stated in this document. It will recognize that it inherits, from episcopal and non-episcopal churches alike, a variety of traditions about the ministry of oversight, unity, and continuity. It will seek to appropriate these traditions creatively, and so to move toward an episcopate reformed and always open to further reformation in the light of the gospel: an episcopate which will probably be different from that now known in any of the covenanting bodies.

50) The service for the ordination of bishops will be in the form of a renewal of the commitment implicit in the person's Baptism and will include prayer for the Holy Spirit with the laying on of hands and an appointment of the bishop to the task of ministry to which he or she has been called.

51) The ministry of bishops, like all other ministries in the Church Uniting, will be at once personal, collegial, and communal, and set within an appropriate constitutional or canonical framework. Bishops of the Church carry out their ministries in a variety of ways. They minister as:

[a] *Liturgical Leaders*. Bishops have responsibility for maintaining the apostolicity and unity of the worship and sacramental life of the Church.

[b] *Teachers of the Apostolic Faith*. Bishops have a responsibility, corporately and individually, to guard, transmit, teach, and proclaim the apostolic faith as it is expressed in Scriptures and Tradition, and, as they are led and endowed by the Spirit, to interpret that faith evangelically and prophetically in the contemporary world.

[c] *Pastoral Overseers*. Bishops have general pastoral oversight of all the people of the dioceses, districts, or jurisdictions to which they are called or appointed. They have particular responsibility, as shepherds, for other ordained ministers. Bishops are responsible for furthering the spiritual unity of their areas, for being available in as wide a range of personal relationships as possible, and for regular visitation of parishes, congregations, and communities in their districts. In such visitations, bishops will ordinarily preach, celebrate the Lord's Supper with the people, and preside at services of Baptism, confirmation, and the ordination of deacons within the congregation.

Ordinarily, responsibility for administration of church discipline, especially as it applies to ordained ministers, will rest with the bishops — but always as they work in cooperation with presbyters, deacons, and lay persons in representative groups which have been given such responsibility.

[d] *Leaders in Mission.* It is an essential task of bishops, both collegially and individually, to further the mission of God's People in Christ to the whole world, in evangelizing, fostering, and nurturing communities of faith and in clarifying the demand for social justice which is directly involved in that mission. In company with other ministers, they take initiative in evolving new approaches for mission wherever they serve.

[e] *Representative Ministers in the Act of Ordination.* Bishops, with the participation of other ministers ordained and unordained, are responsible for the orderly transfer of ministerial authority in the Church. This means not only that bishops preside at ordinations, but also that they share pastoral and administrative responsibility for candidates for the ordained ministry (Acts 8:18; II Tim. 1:6; I Tim. 5:22).

[f] *Administrative Leaders.* Bishops also have responsibility for the supervision and administration of the Church's organized life and work (I Cor. 12:28; Eph. 4:11-12). In the context of the Church assemblies, bishops, as chief pastors, have either directly or by delegation, and always in cooperation with other officers of the Church, a central role in the development of administrative policy and are responsible for the effective carrying out of such policy.

[g] *Servants of Unity.* As personal representatives of the given unity of the Church in all places and all ages, bishops have, both individually and collegially, an obligation "to call the churches to the goal of visible unity in one faith and one eucharistic fellowship expressed in worship and in common life in Christ, and to advance toward that unity that the world may believe" (Constitution of the WCC, III, Functions & Purposes, i).

[h] *Participants in Governance.* As ministers serving within relationships of accountability, bishops have responsibility for taking their constitutionally or canonically defined role, alongside lay persons, presbyters, and deacons, in the governance of the Church.

The Ministry of Presbyters*

52) Presbyters are baptized members of the People of God ordained to serve among the People as ministers of Word and sacraments. In this role they bear responsibility for the discipline of the Church and are teachers and preachers of the faith to the end both that the world may believe and that the entire membership of the Church may be renewed, equipped, and strengthened in its ministry.

---

*Presbyter is a biblical name for persons today designated pastors, elders, ministers, or priests.

53) All presbyters will be ordained by the Church through bishops, with the participation of other presbyters, deacons, and lay persons. The service of presbyteral ordination will be in the form of a renewal of the commitment to ministry implicit in the person's Baptism, and will include prayer for the gift of the Holy Spirit, with the laying on of hands, and an appointment of the presbyter to the task of ministry to which he or she has been called.

54) The presbyteral ministry is personal, collegial, and communal in character and is set within an appropriate constitutional or canonical framework. Presbyters personally represent to the Church its identity in mission in Christ. At the same time, presbyters are associated together in a corporate concern for life and government of the Church under the Word of God (Acts 15:2). Therefore they participate in decision-making assemblies of the Church in which all ministries, lay and ordained, are represented.

55) In order to provide the ministry of Word and sacrament to specific congregations or particular circumstances, the ministry of presbyter may include women and men who, in view of their fitness for this service are chosen, approved, and ordained for such ministry without either leaving their occupations outside the organized structure of the Church or undergoing the normal educational preparation for ordained ministry. Normally the exercise of ministry in these cases will be limited to particular settings, and will require periodic review.

56) Presbyters, in virtue of their calling as ministers of Word and sacraments, serve the Church in a variety of ways. With allowance made for differing circumstances and specialized ministries, the functions of presbyters include the following:

[a] *Preachers of the Word.* Presbyters have a responsibility to proclaim the prophetic and apostolic word of the redemption and liberation wrought by God in Christ (Acts 6:2-4; Eph. 4:11; I Cor. 14:3; I Tim. 4:13-14).

[b] *Celebrants of the Sacraments.* Presbyters normally baptize and preside at the celebration of the Eucharist as recognized representatives of the Church's ministry in Christ, and thus offer, with all the people, spiritual sacrifices acceptable to God (I Peter 2:5). They also bear responsibility for other acts of the Church which for some have a sacramental nature, such as confirmation, marriage, ordination, declaration of the forgiveness of sin, anointing of the sick, and the announcement of God's blessing (VI:19). And they perform or make provision for funeral services and other rites of the Church.

[c] *Teachers of the Gospel.* Presbyters bear responsibility within and outside congregations for teaching the apostolic faith and for handing on the doctrine, discipline, and worship of the Church. They have particular responsibility for the preparation of members for Christian life and ministry. Presbyters may be called to teach in seminaries, divinity schools, theological colleges, and universities, to counsel students and to engage in scholarly research.

[d] *Pastoral Overseers*. Presbyters have responsibility under the Word of God for the pastoral care of persons. This includes spiritual direction of Church members, pastoral use of the Church's disciplines, counseling the troubled, and caring for the sick and needy. Since the members of the congregation have their own part to play in this pastoral ministry, it is the presbyter's responsibility to see that they are not only equipped for mutual pastoral care, but encouraged and enabled to carry it out. Such pastoral ministry has as its aim to nurture the unity and witness of the congregation. Presbyters may serve pastorally also in such settings as the hospital chaplaincy, the counseling center, the campus ministry, and so on.

[e] *Pastoral Administrators*. It is a responsibility of presbyters, when they are serving as leaders of congregations, to see that the many other ministries carried on in the congregation are adequately planned, prepared, and performed, and helped with every resource and support which the congregation can provide. Presbyters may also function as administrators in church boards, agencies, and organizations of all kinds, including ecumenical organizations.

[f] *Leaders in Mission*. Mission is a responsibility of all who share the ministry of Christ. Presbyters, accordingly, are called to leadership in mission. As evangelists they proclaim the gospel, teach God's purposes, and share their personal faith. They bear witness to God's work in the world as well as in the Church. They lead the Church in calling persons to faith in Jesus Christ, and in establishing congregations. As ministers of Word and sacraments, they pioneer in new forms of mission. They enlist, renew, equip, and accompany God's People as they go out into the local community, the nation, and the world.

[g] *Servants of Unity*. As representative ministers of the Church, presbyters work ecumenically across the walls that continue to divide the one Church of Jesus Christ. Specifically it is important for them, by their personal relationships and leadership, to facilitate a vital communion with persons, congregations, and communities of other traditions. At the same time it is their responsibility to give active support and leadership to ecumenical worship, programs, coalitions, councils, and church unions in their local community and, as opportunity may come, at the levels of the region, the nation, and the world (Acts 15:2; II Cor. 8:1-4, 20).

[h] *Participants in Governance*. As ministers serving within relationships of accountability, presbyters have responsibility for taking their constitutionally or canonically defined role, alongside lay persons, bishops, and deacons, in the governance of the Church.

The Ministry of Deacons

57) Deacons are baptized members of the People of God, ordained to represent to the People its identity in Christ as a body of persons who are in

service both to Church and world. It belongs to diaconal ministry to struggle with the myriad needs of societies and persons in Christ's name, and so to exemplify the interdependence of worship and mission in the life of the Church.

58) The nature of the diaconal ministry is classically symbolized by the special role of the deacon in worship. The deacon is the People's helper or servant as he or she is reader and proclaimer of the gospel, leader in intercession, presenter of the Church's offerings to God, minister of the eucharistic bread and wine, and organizer and guide for the People's worship.

59) This liturgical role of the deacon, in turn, finds its proper daily expression in a pastoral function of service and of helping directed to all who seek or need assistance. To the deacon is assigned a special role in the Church's ministry of teaching, in its assistance to those in need of any sort, and in its witness in the world on behalf of the forgotten, the oppressed, and the suffering. With these functions the deacon also assumes a special role in the guidance, focusing, and administration of the Church's ministry of service.

60) The uniting churches recognize that the diaconal ministry has been exercised in a variety of ways at different times and places. This ministry, as a proper and independent ministry in its own right, with its own place in the governance, worship, and pastoral work of the Church, has for long been neglected or suppressed in almost all organized Christian bodies, including the denominations which are members of this Consultation. No doubt there are, in each of our bodies, vestiges of, or surrogates for, the diaconal ministry which in earlier times was central at once to the Church's self-understanding and to its work of shepherding and of witness. On these remains, slight as they may be, a Church Uniting will build with a view to achieving a full restoration of the diaconal office and order in a form suited to the needs and circumstances of the present time.

61) To undertake this work of restoration and reformation will require serious research, imaginative thought, and mutual consultation. This document cannot, therefore, specify ahead of time the exact form of a restored diaconate, or delineate the changes and reforms that a revitalization of the diaconate would entail for the churches.

62) There are, however, certain principles which can be used to guide any consultation to this end. Like all other ministries in and of the Church, the diaconate is at once personal, collegial, and constitutional. It is a ministry in its own right and not a stepping-stone to other offices. It is a ministry which has its basis in the worship, work, and witness of the local church, alongside and together with the ministries of presbyter, layperson, and bishop. It is neither "special," marginal, supplementary, or compensatory. It has its place in the governance and administration of the Church's affairs as well as in its worship and service. There is a tradition in the Church which views the deacon as having a special relation to the bishop.

63) All deacons should represent and take leadership in the general

diaconal responsibility of the congregation in which they worship. Some deacons will serve full-time or part-time in the employ of the Church, working out their particular diaconal callings through the duties they are called upon by the Church to do. Such deacons could come to be called "regular" deacons, after the traditional use of the word to mean "according to rule." Other deacons will work out their particular callings in the world, in and through their activities in commerce, industry, education, government, the professions, and the like. These deacons will model for other Christians ways and means of fulfilling their "secular" or "in-the-world" calling to serve Jesus Christ and could thus come to be called "secular deacons," again adapting the traditional usage. Some deacons may change, according to need, from "regular" to "secular" status, or vice-versa. All deacons, whatever their place or status of ministry, will serve in the following ways:

[a] *Servants in Worship*. Deacons, whatever their particular arenas of activity, normally participate as leaders in the worship within local congregations. It is their responsibility to read the Scriptures, including the Gospel, preaching when called to do so, leading the assembled people in prayer, assisting in the administration of the sacraments.

[b] *Partners in Congregational Oversight*. Upon election by a congregation for that purpose, deacons share in the oversight of ministry of that congregation. Together with presbyters and lay persons, such deacons will be concerned with the discipline and deployment of their congregations as collective expressions of the gospel.

[c] *Participants in Governance*. As ministers serving within relationships of accountability, deacons have responsibility for taking their constitutionally or canonically defined role, alongside lay persons, bishops, and presbyters, in the governance of the Church.

[d] *Leaders in Administration*. Deacons carry administrative responsibility in the life of the Church. The "gift of administration," seen in the New Testament as a pastoral gift, is an indispensable ministry among the People of God for which deacons may be specially suited.

[e] *Leaders in Mission*. Deacons may carry a responsibility for the development of mission both within and beyond parishes and congregations. Some may find the focus of their ministry primarily in their regular employment. Some may be volunteers with regular responsibilities in mission.

[f] *Servants in Pastoral Care*. Deacons may have a responsible share in the Church's concern for the pastoral care of persons. This includes not only their traditional responsibility for the care of the sick and needy but also a responsibility for the spiritual life of the congregation and its discipline.

[g] *Servants of Unity*. With their special concern for mission in the world, deacons may be called to witness to the unity of humankind in Christ by bringing the Church into dialogue with the society in which it is set. In the midst of diversity, they further, through their witness, the practical acknowledgement of human community.

Theology Commission
1980-1984

African Methodist Episcopal Church	Dr. William P. DeVeaux
African Methodist Episcopal Zion Church	Professor George B. Thomas
Christian Church (Disciples of Christ)	Dr. James O. Duke
Christian Methodist Episcopal Church	Dr. Thomas Hoyt, Jr.
Episcopal Church	Professor Richard A. Norris
International Council of Community Churches	Dr. Jeffrey Newhall
Presbyterian Church (USA)	Dr. Cynthia Campbell
Chairperson	Dean Lewis S. Mudge
United Church of Christ	Dr. Reuben Sheares, II
United Methodist Church	Dr. J. Robert Nelson

At-large Members

The Rev. Page Bigelow
The Rev. William Hulteen
The Rev. Carroll Kann
Professor Richard Lovelace
Dr. Harold Wilke

Observer/Consultants	
Lutheran Council in the USA	Dr. Joseph A. Burgess
Reformed Church in America	Dr. James Van Hoeven
Roman Catholic Church	Professor John T. Ford
Adjunct Staff Team Member	Dr. Robert K. Welsh
Secretariat	Dr. Gerald F. Moede
	The Rev. John E. Brandon (1980-81)
	Dr. William D. Watley (1982-84)